Paul Romanuk

SCHOLASTIC CANADA

BOOK OF HOCKEY LISTS

Illustrations by Bill Dickson

Scholastic Canada Ltd.
Toronto New York London Auckland Sydney
Mexico City New Delhi Hong Kong Buenos Aires

In memory of Barb and Ed, my mom and dad, who helped me to learn to love this game, and also to Tim, the brother I never had, who still loves to talk about how great the 1970s Montreal Canadiens were.

Much of the material in this book came from my own notes and research; however, I would also like to acknowledge, in no particular order, some other great sources of hockey info that helped me out: The Hockey Hall of Fame, NHL.com, the International Ice Hockey Federation, hockeydb.com, Total Hockey, and CHL.com.

This book includes information up to the 2006–2007 season. Some records may change.

Photo Credits:
p. 11: Doug MacLellan/Hockey Hall of Fame
p. 17 and 70: O-Pee-Chee/Hockey Hall of Fame
p. 25: Graphic Artists/Hockey Hall of Fame
p. 30: 74, 138: Dave Sandford/Hockey Hall of Fame
p. 57: Hockey Hall of Fame
p. 61 and 86: Imperial Oil-Turofsky/Hockey Hall of Fame
p. 93: London Life-Portnoy/Hockey Hall of Fame
p. 99: Robert Shaver/Hockey Hall of Fame

Library and Archives Canada Cataloguing in Publication
Romanuk, Paul
Scholastic Canada book of hockey lists / Paul Romanuk, author.

ISBN 978-0-439-93562-3

1. Hockey--Miscellanea--Juvenile literature. I. Title. II. Title: Book of hockey lists.

GV847.25.R64 2007   j796.962   C2007-901040-7

ISBN-10 0-439-93562-8

INTRODUCTION

When I was around 14 years old, I lived for hockey. I collected hockey cards, kept scrapbooks of teams and players, watched Dave Hodge on *Hockey Night in Canada* and listened to the great Danny Gallivan call play-by-play. But mostly, I remember the days spent in the school library with my friends — Tim, Butch, John and Ted — poring over old copies of *The Hockey News*, *Hockey Pictorial* and *Hockey World*, trying to memorize every stat from every story.

"Hey, did you know Bobby Orr started playing in Oshawa when he was 14?"

"Really? When did he score his first goal?"

"I don't know, but he didn't always wear number four, you know."

"Yeah, I knew that." (Which would always be the answer, even if you didn't know).

I guess that's why I've always wanted to do a book of hockey lists with a little more than just the regular lists you always see, like goals, assists and total points. Those lists are here, but I've also included things like colossal contracts, countries where they play more hockey than you'd think, and even players with the greatest mustaches of all time. It was fun to track down those fun facts — it took me back to those days in the school library, books, magazines and newspapers laid out in front of me, school books pushed to the side for the time being, totally immersed in hockey. I hope you can get the same enjoyment out of this book as I did from the hockey books I did back when I was a kid.

Cheers,

Paul

By the numbers

761 The number of game passes, season passes, field passes, dressing room passes and other types of accreditation I have sitting in a box inside my closet

CONTENTS

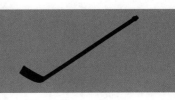

MILESTONES

Big and small numbers from some of the greatest individuals and teams ever to take to the ice.

MOST GOALS IN A SEASON

92	Wayne Gretzky	**1981–82**
87	Wayne Gretzky	**1983–84**
86	Brett Hull	**1990–91**
85	Mario Lemieux	**1988–89**
76	Phil Esposito	**1970–71**
	Alexander Mogilny	**1992–93**
	Teemu Selanne	**1992–93**

103 Number of days NHL owners locked out players during the labour dispute during the 1994–95 season. Teams only played 48 games that season.

MOST CAREER GOALS

Wayne Gretzky	**894**
Gordie Howe	**801**
Brett Hull	**741**
Marcel Dionne	**731**
Phil Esposito	**717**
Mike Gartner	**708**
Mark Messier	**694**
Steve Yzerman	**692**
Mario Lemieux	**690**
Luc Robitaille	**668**

MOST POINTS IN A SEASON

The Great One is the only player in NHL history to score 200 or more points in a season. While he was playing for the Edmonton Oilers, Wayne Gretzky recorded the four highest single-season points totals ever:

215 **points**	1985–86
212 **points**	1981–82
208 **points**	1984–85
205 **points**	1983–84

MOST CAREER POINTS

Wayne Gretzky

2857 career points in 20 seasons with Edmonton, Los Angeles, St. Louis and New York Rangers

Mark Messier

1887 career points in 25 seasons with Edmonton, New York Rangers and Vancouver

Gordie Howe

1850 career points in 26 seasons with Detroit and Hartford

Ron Francis

1798 career points in 23 seasons with Hartford, Pittsburgh, Carolina and Toronto

Marcel Dionne

1771 career points in 18 seasons with Detroit, Los Angeles and New York Rangers

MOST HOME WINS IN A SEASON

This is a strange category because the length of the NHL schedule has changed over the years. Teams now play 82 games. But they've also played 80 games, 78, 76, 74, 70, all the way back to as few as 20 games in a season.

36	Philadelphia Flyers	1975–1976
	Detroit Red Wings	1995–1996
33	Boston Bruins	1970–1971
	Boston Bruins	1973–1974
	Montreal Canadiens	1976–1977
	Philadelphia Flyers	1976–1977
	New York Islanders	1981–1982
	Philadelphia Flyers	1985–1986

FEWEST HOME WINS IN A SEASON

Another strange one for the same reason as Most Home Wins in a Season — but still impressive.

2	Chicago Black Hawks	1927–1928
7	Boston Bruins	1924–1925
	Chicago Black Hawks	1928–1929
	Philadelphia Quakers	1930–1931

126 Number of NHL games played in the history of the defunct Hamilton Tigers

7

MOST SHUTOUTS IN A SEASON

Almost all of these totals were recorded back in the 1920s.

22	George Hainsworth, Montreal Canadiens	1928–29*
15	Alex Connell, Ottawa Senators	1925–26 & 1927–28
	Hal Winkler, Boston Bruins	1927–28
	Tony Esposito, Chicago Black Hawks	1969–70
14	George Hainsworth, Montreal Canadiens	1926–27

* An amazing accomplishment, especially since he only played 44 games

25 Number of games without a win that the 1980–81 Winnipeg Jets had to endure. It is the longest winless streak in NHL history.

BIGGEST SINGLE GAME GOAL TOTAL IN CANADIAN HOCKEY LEAGUE (ONE TEAM)

22 January 29, 1978, QMJHL*
Sherbrooke Beavers **22**, Shawinigan Cataractes **4**

20 December 22, 1986, QMJHL
Shawinigan Cataractes **20**, Verdun Canadiens **5**

November 16, 1975, QMJHL
Sherbrooke Beavers **20**, Shawinigan Cataractes **2**

March 18, 1979, QMJHL
Trois-Rivières Draveurs **20**, Laval Nationale **6**

19 February 11, 1984, WHL†
Medicine Hat Tigers **19**, Winnipeg Warriors **2**

November 13, 1987, QMJHL
Shawinigan Cataractes **19**, Verdun Canadiens **2**

October 3, 1990, WHL
Tri-City Americans **19**, Seattle Thunderbirds **3**

17 February 19, 1977, WHL
New Westminster Bruins **17**, Winnipeg Monarchs **0**

16 January 21, 1977, OHL‡
Sault Ste. Marie Greyhounds **16**, Peterborough Petes **6**

December 17, 1978, OHL
Peterborough Petes **16**, Sault Ste. Marie Greyhounds **5**

January 11, 1980, OHL
Ottawa 67s **16**, Brantford Alexanders **6**

* Quebec Major Junior Hockey League
† Western Hockey League
‡ Ontario Hockey League

MOST CAREER SHUTOUTS

103	Terry Sawchuk
94	George Hainsworth
92	Martin Brodeur
84	Glenn Hall
82	Jacques Plante
81	Cecil "Tiny" Thompson
	Alex Connell
76	Tony Esposito
	Ed Belfour
	Dominik Hasek

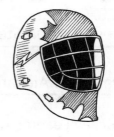

MOST GAMES PLAYED BY A GOALIE

Patrick Roy

1,029 games – Patrick Roy
19 seasons with Montreal and Colorado

971 games – Terry Sawchuk
21 seasons with Detroit, Boston, Toronto, Los Angeles and the New York Rangers

906 games – Glenn Hall
18 seasons with Detroit, Chicago and St. Louis

963 games – Ed Belfour
With Chicago, San Jose, Dallas, Toronto and Florida

886 games – Tony Esposito
15 seasons with Montreal and Chicago

FASTEST GOALS FROM THE START OF A GAME

:05 seconds	Doug Smail, Winnipeg Jets December 20, 1981 vs. St. Louis Blues
	Bryan Trottier, New York Islanders March 22, 1984 vs. Boston Bruins
	Alexander Mogilny, Buffalo Sabres December 21, 1991 vs. Toronto Maple Leafs
:06 seconds	Henry Boucha, Detroit Red Wings January 28, 1973 vs. Montreal Canadiens
	Jean Pronovost, Pittsburgh Penguins March 25, 1976 vs. St. Louis Blues
:07 seconds	Charlie Conacher, Toronto Maple Leafs February 6, 1932 vs. Boston Bruins
	Danny Gare, Buffalo Sabres December 17, 1978 vs. Vancouver Canucks
	Dave "Tiger" Williams, Los Angeles Kings February 14, 1987 vs. Hartford Whalers

GOALIES WITH THE MOST CAREER WINS

551	Patrick Roy
494	Martin Brodeur
484	Ed Belfour
447	Terry Sawchuk
442	Curtis Joseph
437	Jacques Plante
423	Tony Esposito
407	Glenn Hall
403	Grant Fuhr

12 The number of times Wayne Gretzky has been on the cover of *Sports Illustrated*

MOST GOALS BY A DEFENSEMAN

410	Ray Bourque
396	Paul Coffey
340	Al MacInnis
338	Phil Housley
310	Denis Potvin

LONGEST NHL GAMES

116 minutes, 30 seconds — March 24, 1936
Detroit Red Wings 1, Montreal Maroons 0
Game winning goal: Mud Bruneteau

105 minutes, 46 seconds — April 3, 1933
Toronto Maple Leafs 1, Boston Bruins 0
Game winning goal: Ken Doraty

92 minutes, 1 second — May 4, 2000
Philadelphia Flyers 2, Pittsburgh Penguins 1
Game winning goal: Keith Primeau

80 minutes, 48 seconds — April 24, 2003
Anaheim Mighty Ducks 4, Dallas Stars 3
Game winning goal: Petr Sykora

79 minutes, 15 seconds — April 24, 1996
Pittsburgh Penguins 3, Washington Capitals 2
Game winning goal: Petr Nedved

78 minutes, 6 seconds — April 11, 2007
Vancouver Canucks 5, Dallas Stars 4
Game winning goal: Henrik Sedin

70 minutes, 18 seconds — March 23, 1943
Toronto Maple Leafs 3, Detroit Red Wings 2
Game winning goal: Jack McLean

68 minutes, 52 seconds — March 28, 1930
Montreal Canadiens 2, New York Rangers 1
Game winning goal: Gus Rivers

68 minutes, 47 seconds — April 18, 1987
New York Islanders 3, Washington Capitals 2
Game winning goal: Pat LaFontaine

65 minutes, 43 seconds — April 27, 1994
Buffalo Sabres 1, New Jersey Devils 0
Game winning goal: Dave Hannan

HIGHEST POINT TOTALS BY A ROOKIE

132	**Teemu Selanne**, Winnipeg Jets	1992–93
109	**Peter Stastny**, Quebec Nordiques	1980–81
106	**Alexander Ovechkin**, Washington Capitals	
		2005–06
103	**Dale Hawerchuk,** Winnipeg Jets	1981–82
102	**Joe Juneau**, Boston Bruins	1992–93
	Sidney Crosby, Pittsburgh Penguins	2005–06
100	**Mario Lemieux**, Pittsburgh Penguins	1984–85

3,000 The number of people who gathered outside Edmonton's St. Joseph's Basilica during Wayne Gretzky's wedding to actress Janet Jones

MOST GOALS BY A ROOKIE

Teemu Selanne

76	**Teemu Selanne**, Winnipeg Jets	1992–93
53	**Mike Bossy**, New York Islanders	1977–78
52	**Alexander Ovechkin**, Washington Capitals	
		2005–06
51	**Joe Nieuwendyk**, Calgary Flames	1987–88
45	**Dale Hawerchuk**, Winnipeg Jets	1981–82
	Luc Robitaille, Los Angeles Kings	1986–87

HIGHEST SINGLE-SEASON POINT TOTALS (CHL)

282	Mario Lemieux, Laval Voisins QMJHL*, 1983–84 (70 games)
251	Pierre Larouche, Sorel Black Hawks QMJHL, 1973–74 (67 games)
234	Pat Lafontaine, Verdun Juniors QMJHL, 1982–83 (70 games)
227	Michel Deziel, Sorel Black Hawks QMJHL, 1973–74 (69 games)
216	Real Cloutier, Quebec Remparts QMJHL, 1973–74 (68 games)
214	Jacques Cossette, Soral Black Hawks QMJHL*, 1973–74 (68 games)
212	Rob Brown, Kamloops Blazers WHL[†], 1986–87 (72 games)
209	Guy Lafleur, Quebec Remparts QMJHL, 1970–71 (62 games)
206	Jacques Locas, Quebec Remparts QMJHL, 1973–74 (63 games)
201	Marc Fortier, Chicoutimi Saguenéens QMJHL, 1986–87 (65 games)

*Quebec Major Junior Hockey League
[†] Western Hockey League

MOST ASSISTS BY A ROOKIE

70	**Peter Stastny**, Quebec Nordiques	1980–81
	Joe Juneau, Boston Bruins	1992–93
63	**Bryan Trottier**, New York Islanders	1975–76
	Sidney Crosby, Pittsburgh Penguins	2005–06
62	**Sergei Makarov**, Calgary Flames	1989–90
60	**Larry Murphy**, Los Angeles Kings	1980–81

HIGHEST WINNING PERCENTAGE IN A SEASON (CHL)

.882	London Knights, OHL*, 2004–05 (59–7–2 in 68 games)
.879	Quebec Remparts, QMJHL†, 1970–71 (54–7–1 in 62 games)
.868	Brandon Wheat Kings, WHL‡, 1978–79 (58–5–9 in 72 games)
.847	Trois Rivières Draveurs, QMJHL, 1978–79 (58–8–6 in 72 games)
.840	Victoria Cougars, WHL, 1980–81 (60–11–1 in 72 games)
.836	Sorel Éperviers, QMJHL, 1973–74 (58–11–1 in 70 games)
.826	Prince Albert Raiders, WHL, 1984–85 (58–11–3 in 72 games)
	Sault Ste. Marie Greyhounds, OHL, 1984–85 (54–11–1 in 66 games)

* Ontario Hockey League
† Quebec Major Junior Hockey League
‡ Western Hockey League

MOST CAREER PENALTY MINUTES
(REGULAR SEASON)

3,966	**Dave "Tiger" Williams**	1974–75 to 1987–88*
3,565	**Dale Hunter**	1980–81 to 1998–99
3,515	**Tie Domi**	1989–90 to 2005–06
3,381	**Marty McSorley**	1983–84 to 1999–2000†
3,300	**Bob Probert**	1985–86 to 2001–02
3,207	**Rob Ray**	1989–90 to 2003–04
3,149	**Craig Berube**	1986–87 to 2002–03
3,146	**Tim Hunter**	1981–82 to 1996–97‡
3,043	**Chris Nilan**	1979–80 to 1991–92
2,972	**Rick Tocchet**	1984–85 to 2001–02

* That's almost three days, non-stop, sitting in the penalty box.
† Many of those minutes were gathered protecting teammate Wayne Gretzky.
‡ Tim and Dale are brothers. Wonder if brotherly quarrels at the Hunter household were fairly common?

MOST PENALTIES IN

10 – Chris Nilan
Boston Bruins vs. Hartford Whalers, March 31, 1991: 6 minors, 2 majors, a 10-minute misconduct and 1 game misconduct.

9 – Jim Dorey
Toronto Maple Leafs vs. Pittsburgh Penguins, October 16, 1968: 4 minors, 2 majors, 2 10-minute misconducts, 1 game misconduct.

9 – Dave "The Hammer" Schultz
Pittsburgh Penguins vs. Detroit Red Wings, April 6, 1978: 5 minors, 2 majors, 2 10-minute misconducts.

9 – Randy Holt
Los Angeles Kings vs. Philadelphia Flyers, March 11, 1979: 1 minor, 3 majors, 2 10-minute misconducts, 3 game misconducts.

9 – Russ Anderson
Pittsburgh Penguins vs. Edmonton Oilers, January 19, 1980: 3 minors, 3 majors, 3 game misconducts.

A SINGLE GAME

9 – Kim Clackson

Quebec Nordiques vs. Chicago Blackhawks, March 8, 1981:
4 minors, 3 majors, 2 game misconducts.

9 – Terry O'Reilly

Boston Bruins vs. Hartford Whalers, December 19, 1984: 5 minors,
3 majors, 1 game misconduct.

9 – Larry Playfair

Los Angeles Kings vs. New York Islanders, December 9, 1986:
6 minors, 2 majors, 1 10-minute misconduct.

9 – Marty McSorley

Los Angeles Kings vs. Vancouver Canucks, April 14, 1992: 5 minors,
2 majors, 1 10-minute misconduct, 1 game misconduct.

9 – Reed Low

St. Louis Blues vs. Detroit Red Wings, December 31, 2002: 4 minors,
1 major, 1 10-minute misconduct, 3 game misconducts.

HIGHEST SINGLE-SEASON GOAL TOTALS (CHL)

133	Mario Lemieux, Laval Voisins QMJHL*, 1983–84 (70 games)
130	Guy Lafleur, Quebec Remparts QMJHL, 1970–71 (62 games)
108	Ray Ferraro, Brandon Wheat Kings WHL†, 1983–84 (72 games)
104	Pat Lafontaine, Verdun Juniors QMJHL 1982–83 (70 games)
103	Guy Lafleur, Quebec Remparts QMJHL, 1969–70 (56 games)
100	Gary MacGregor, Cornwall Royals QMJHL, 1973–74 (66 games)
99	Jacques Locas, Quebec Remparts QMJHL, 1973–74 (67 games)
97	Jacques Cossette, Sorel Black Hawks QMJHL, 1973–74 (68 games)
96	Bill Derlago, Brandon Wheat Kings WHL, 1976–77 (72 games)
94	Pierre Larouche, Sorel Black Hawks QMJHL, 1973–74 (67 games)

* Quebec Major Junior Hockey League
† Western Hockey League

MOST CAREER FIRST OR SECOND ALL-STAR TEAM SELECTIONS

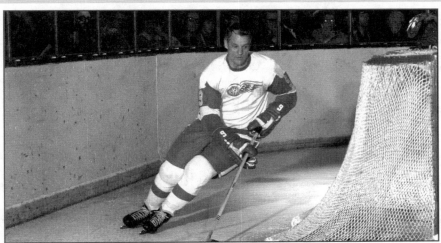

Gordie Howe

21	Gordie Howe	12 First Team, 9 Second Team
19	Ray Bourque	13 First Team, 6 Second Team
15	Wayne Gretzky	8 First Team, 7 Second Team
14	Maurice "The Rocket" Richard	8 First Team, 6 Second Team
12	Bobby Hull	10 First Team, 2 Second Team
11	Glenn Hall	7 First Team, 4 Second Team
	Doug Harvey	10 First Team, 1 Second Team
10	Jean Beliveau	6 First Team, 4 Second Team
	Earl Seibert	4 First Team, 6 Second Team
9	Bobby Orr	8 First Team, 1 Second Team
	Ted Lindsay	8 First Team, 1 Second Team
	Frank Mahovlich	3 First Team, 6 Second Team
	Mario Lemieux	5 First Team, 4 Second Team

MOST ALL-STAR TEAM SELECTIONS BY POSITION

GOAL	Glenn Hall	**11**
DEFENSE	Ray Bourque	**19**
	Doug Harvey	**11**
LEFT WING	Bobby Hull	**12**
CENTRE	Wayne Gretzky	**15**
RIGHT WING	Gordie Howe	**21**

89.54 The height, in centimetres, of the Stanley Cup

TOP CAREER GOAL TOTALS (CHL)

309	Mike Bossy Laval Nationale, QMJHL*	
281	Stephan Lebeau Shawinigan Cataractes, QMJHL	
278	Normand Dupont Montreal Red-White-Blue / Juniors, QMJHL	
269	Jacques Locas St. Jerome Alouettes / Quebec Remparts, QMJHL*	
262	Glen Goodall Seattle Breakers / Thunderbirds, WHL†	
261	Ron Chipperfield Brandon Wheat Kings, WHL	
258	Normand Aubin Sorel / Verdun Black Hawks / Sherbrooke Beavers, QMJHL	
254	Sylvain Locas Chicoutimi Saguenéens / Sherbrooke Beavers, QMJHL	
252	Guy Rouleau Longueuil Chevaliers, Hull Olympiques, QMJHL	
247	Mario Lemieux Laval Voisins, QMJHL	

* Quebec Major Junior Hockey League
† Western Hockey League

HIGHEST CAREER POINT TOTALS (CHL)

595   Patrice Lefebvre
          Shawinigan Cataractes, QMJHL*

591   Brian Sakic
          Swift Current Broncos, Tri-City Americans, WHL†

580   Stephan Lebeau
          Shawinigan Cataractes, QMJHL

575   Patrick Emond
          Trois-Rivières Draveurs, Hull Olympiques,
          Chicoutimi Sagueneens, QMJHL

573   Glen Goodall
          Seattle Breakers / Thunderbirds, WHL

568   Normand Dupont
          Montreal Red-White-Blue / Juniors, QMJHL

562   Mario Lemieux
          Laval Voisins, QMJHL

558   Jacques Locas
          St. Jerome Alouettes, Quebec Remparts, QMJHL

545   Sylvain Locas
          Chicoutimi Saguenéens, Sherbrooke Beavers, QMJHL

543   Guy Rouleau
          Longueuil Chevaliers, Hull Olympiques, QMJHL

* Quebec Major Junior Hockey League
† Western Hockey League

DID YOU KNOW ?

First game with artificial ice . . . celebrity hockey fans . . .
how much Howie Morenz made in 1924 — it's all here.

HARDEST SHOTS

This is a tough one to measure. Bernie "Boom Boom" Geoffrion is credited with inventing the slapshot during his years with the Montreal Canadiens in the 1950s and '60s. But there have been many other players goalies have dreaded to face.

Brett Hull

1. Al Iafrate*

2. Al MacInnis†

3. Sergei Fedorov

4. Fredrik Modin

5. Jaromir Jagr

6. Alexei Kovalev

7. Bill Guerin

8. Rob Blake

9. Eric Lindros

10. Jarome Iginla

11. Brett Hull

* His shot was clocked at a record-setting 169 kilometres per hour!

† Won the hardest-shot competition at the NHL All-Star Game seven times. One season he broke the catching hands of two opposition goalies with his blazing shot.

COLOSSAL CONTRACTS

Like most things we pay for in life, employing a professional hockey player has become more and more expensive over the years. But the best players have always made a lot more money than the average person who pays to watch them play.

- Howie Morenz   *$3,500 1923–24

- Bobby Hull $1,000,000 1977–78

- Wayne Gretzky $6,545,400 1995–96

- Mats Sundin $9,000,000 2003–04

- Jaromir Jagr $11,483,333 2002–03

* The average annual salary in Canada at that time was about $960.

MAJOR EQUIPMENT INNOVATIONS

Artificial Ice

Where would the game be without artificial ice? Most definitely not in Florida, Dallas, California, Vancouver or a host of other places. It's believed the first hockey game played on artificial ice was in late December of 1894 in Baltimore between Johns Hopkins University and Baltimore Athletic Club.

Goalie pads

In the early days of hockey, goalies wore the same equipment as the other players. A few smart goalies started wearing the same pads that cricket batsmen wore. In the early 1920s a horse harness maker in Hamilton, Ontario, "Pop" Kenesky, made the first "oversized" leather pads (stuffed with deer hair, because it is lighter than horse hair). These pads became a fixture of goalie equipment for the next 50 years until pads started to be made from lighter materials that didn't soak up moisture from the ice, which makes them heavier.

Goalie masks

Montreal Canadiens goaltender Jacques Plante made wearing goalie masks acceptable in NHL games after he donned one in a famous game on November 1, 1959. Since then the mask has continued to evolve — better material, angles that deflect the impact of a stick or puck — to the point where facial injuries for goalies are almost non-existent.

Helmets

Most players didn't wear head protection until it was made compulsory in the 1970s for players in college or junior hockey. The NHL decreed that "any player signing a contract after June 1, 1979 must wear a helmet." Early helmets were made of leather and felt. Today's helmets are engineering marvels that save countless players from cuts and concussions.

Visors

Visors, partial or full-face, have only been popular since the late 1970s when the International Ice Hockey Federation mandated that all junior players had to wear a half-visor. This rule was modified in 1978 to include a full face shield. Since the rule changes, the number of players in Canada suffering an eye injury or blindness while wearing the protection properly is down to 3 or 4 a year — from over 250 thirty years ago. Sadly, most NHL players still don't wear visors.

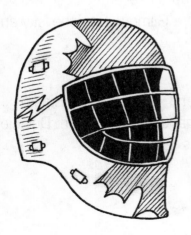

CELEBRITY HOCKEY FANS

Seems like everyone loves hockey. Here are a few famous fans.

▬▬ Kiefer Sutherland

The star of the TV series *24* grew up in Canada playing and loving the game. He's even done some TV commercials for the NHL and calls Wayne Gretzky a good friend.

▬▬ Keanu Reeves

Before becoming "The One" in the *Matrix* movies, Reeves held a job sharpening skates, and also played high school hockey while growing up in Toronto. He was a goalie and was named MVP of his team. He also picked up the nickname "The Wall."

▬▬ Mike Myers

Mike Myers, a.k.a. Austin Powers, International Man of Mystery, is a huge Toronto Maple Leafs fan. He's made several references to the team in his movies over the years: during a newscast in *Austin Powers in Goldmember* the ticker at the bottom of the screen says, "Maple Leafs win Stanley Cup." He's also shown up on several talk shows wearing his jersey, and his dogs' names are Gilmour, Borschevsky and, of course, 99.

▬▬ Gord Downie

The lead singer of the iconic Canadian band The Tragically Hip is the godson of former Boston general manager Harry Sinden. Downie plays goal himself and is a big-time Bruins fan.

Avril Lavigne

Apparently Lavigne was a bit of a fan while she was growing up in Napanee, Ontario. She's been known to suit up and head out for a game of shinny while she's out on tour. She even did a cover version of "The Hockey Song."

Denis Leary

The well-known television actor and comedian grew up in Worcester, Massachusetts, and started a life-long love of hockey and the Boston Bruins. Leary played hockey while he was growing up, and wanted to play in the NHL one day. These days he settles for the odd pickup game and charity games.

Shania Twain

The singing superstar is from Timmins, Ontario, and has been known to pop up on stage wearing a hockey sweater.

John Ondrasik

The man behind the band Five For Fighting (a hockey term, as in "five minutes for fighting") is buddies with Wayne Gretzky and Luc Robitaille. He's a big Los Angeles Kings fan.

Garth Brooks

The country music legend started getting into the game after the Nashville Predators showed up on the scene. He's been a fan ever since, and is a regular at home games when he's not on tour.

PRE-GAME MEALS

Some pre-game favourites . . .

■ Chicken and pasta

By far the most popular. Usually the chicken is steamed or baked and the pasta is spaghetti with a tomato-based sauce.

■ Chicken with vegetables

A close second. Rather than the pasta, some players like the traditional potatoes (steamed, boiled or baked) and carrots or broccoli.

■ Steak and pasta

Not as popular as it would have been 40 years ago. Back then it was the pre-game meal of choice among almost all athletes.

■ Soup, sandwich and a green salad

Many prefer a very light meal before the game and something more substantial afterward. The kind of soup varies, but the most common sandwiches tend to be tuna or chicken.

■ Energy bar or shake

More and more athletes take in the calories and vitamins they need with a specially designed energy drink or one of the popular over-the-counter energy bars.

HOCKEY PLAYERS
WHO ARE GOOD AT OTHER SPORTS

Lionel Conacher*	Baseball, lacrosse
Wayne Gretzky	Baseball, lacrosse
Pierre Larouche	Golf
Grant Fuhr	Golf
Joe Nieuwendyk†	Lacrosse
Gary Roberts	Lacrosse
Bucko McDonald	Lacrosse
Adam Oates	Lacrosse
Hayley Wickenheiser‡	Fastball
Rikka Nieminen	Fastball

* Voted Canada's outstanding male athlete of the half-century (1900–50)

† The only person to ever win the MVP award in both the Stanley Cup and the Minto Cup (lacrosse)

‡ The first woman to ever compete in both summer and winter Olympics in team sports

MORE EQUIPMENT INNOVATIONS

Neck protection

Until the late 1970s neck protection was an afterthought for most players. The original "Crouch Collar" was designed by the father of a goalie named Kim Crouch who suffered a horrific cut on his neck from a skate blade during a minor hockey game. Quick thinking by the trainer stopped Crouch from bleeding to death. Virtually all goalies and all minor hockey players now wear a version of this collar.

Skates

In the late 1970s companies started moving away from the traditional tube skate — various tubes of metal fitted together and holding the blade in place at the bottom of the skate boot. During the 1978 season a few Montreal players started using the Tuuk blade. Rather than tube steel at the bottom of the boot, there was much lighter hard plastic with a small, thin blade fastened into the plastic. This design has remained virtually unchanged and is the standard in all hockey skates.

Pads

Felt and leather were the main materials for almost all pads until after the Second World War and the invention of plastics and fibreglass. Since then the innovation has been constant — harder and even lighter materials (like Kevlar) give players amazing protection from pucks and sticks and heavy collisions.

Safety glass

There was a time when the only protection for fans from flying pucks was a big metal screen in each end zone. It didn't make for the best viewing for the fans sitting in the expensive seats. With the invention of Plexiglas and, later, shatterproof glass, this problem was solved. Amazingly, many rinks didn't add protective glass along the sides until the early 1960s. Until then it wasn't uncommon for fans in the front row to be hit by a puck or clipped by a stick.

Stick

No basic piece of hockey equipment has evolved as much as the stick. Back in 1900 sticks were handmade from a single piece of wood. Sticks later became two-piece, with the blade and the shaft made from different parts of the tree. Later came curved sticks, fibreglass-wrapped sticks, layered shafts, metal shafts and now, the one-piece stick made of graphite.

DEVELOPMENT LEAGUES
YOUNG PLAYERS ARE DRAFTED FROM

- Ontario Hockey League — 22%

- Europe, Nordic nations, Russia / Commonwealth of Independent States / Soviet Union — 20%

- Western Hockey League — 19%

- College hockey — 12%

- Quebec Major Junior Hockey League — 10%

- U.S. high school hockey — 8%

- Other — 9%

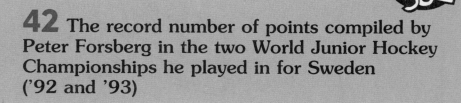

By the numbers

42 The record number of points compiled by Peter Forsberg in the two World Junior Hockey Championships he played in for Sweden ('92 and '93)

TOP TEN JUNIOR TEAMS THAT SUPPLY PLAYERS TO THE NHL DRAFT

Peterborough Petes, Ontario Hockey League

Oshawa Generals, Ontario Hockey League

London Knights, Ontario Hockey League

Kitchener Rangers, Ontario Hockey League

Ottawa 67s, Ontario Hockey League

Sudbury Wolves, Ontario Hockey League

Sault Ste. Marie Greyhounds, Ontario Hockey League

Kamloops Blazers, Western Hockey League

Regina Pats, Western Hockey League

Medicine Hat Tigers, Western Hockey League

TOP TEN COLLEGE TEAMS THAT SUPPLY PLAYERS TO THE NHL DRAFT

Minnesota Gophers

Michigan Wolverines

Boston University Terriers

Michigan State Spartans

Michigan Tech Huskies

Denver Pioneers

Wisconsin Badgers

North Dakota Fighting Sioux

Boston College Eagles

Providence Friars

TOP TEN INTERNATIONAL TEAMS THAT SUPPLY PLAYERS TO THE NHL DRAFT

■ CSKA Moscow (Red Army), Russia

■ Dynamo Moscow, Russia

■ HIFK Helsinki, Finland

■ Djurgarden, Sweden

■ Vasta Frolunda, Sweden

■ MoDo, Sweden

■ Jokerit, Finland

■ Chemo Litvinov, Czech Republic

■ TPS Turku, Finland

■ Farjestad, Sweden

FIRST NUMBER-ONE DRAFT PICKS

1. **Gary Monahan, 1963** – Taken by the Montreal Canadiens from the St. Michael's Juveniles in Toronto; played 748 NHL games over 12 seasons and had 285 points

2. **Claude Gauthier, 1964** – Drafted by Detroit; never played a single game in the NHL

3. **Andre Veilleux, 1965** – First pick of the New York Rangers; also never played an NHL game

4. **Barry Gibbs, 1966** – A defenseman taken by the Boston Bruins; played 13 NHL seasons (a total of 797 games) and had 282 points

5. **Rick Pagnutti, 1967** – Taken by the Los Angeles Kings in their first NHL Draft; never played in the NHL

6. **Michel Plasse, 1968** – First goaltender ever drafted first overall; was chosen by the Montreal Canadiens and played 299 games over 11 seasons in the NHL

7. **Rejean Houle, 1969** – Left winger had a spectacular career with the team that drafted him, the Montreal Canadiens; was on 5 Stanley Cup-winning teams

(AND HOW THEY DID)

8. **Gilbert Perreault, 1970** – Famously drafted by Buffalo after the spin of a wheel between the Sabres and their fellow expansion team entry Vancouver; went on to be one of the top NHL centremen of his era, playing 1191 career games with Buffalo and scoring 1326 points

9. **Guy Lafleur, 1971** – Montreal Canadiens' general manager Sam Pollock did everything he could, wheeling and dealing to make sure the Habs had the first overall pick; "The Flower" was part of the Montreal dynasty in the 1970s, helping them win 5 Stanley Cups

10. **Billy Harris, 1972** – The first draft pick ever for the expansion New York Islanders; played 12 seasons in the NHL and finished with 558 points in 897 games

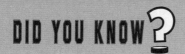
NHL PLAYERS
WHO WORE GLASSES ON THE ICE

In this era of laser eye surgery and contact lenses, wearing glasses is unheard of, but there was a time . . .

Clint Albright
Al Arbour
John Vanbiesbrouck
Russ Blinco
Steve Carlson

48 The number of players with the last name "Smith" who have played at least one game in the NHL

MOST COMMON NHL LAST NAMES

◆ Smith

◆ Johnson

◆ Martin

◆ Morrison

◆ Hill

◆ Jones

◆ Tremblay

◆ Boucher

◆ Johansson

◆ Anderson or Andersson*

* The first spelling is more common in North America;
  the second is a Swedish spelling of the same name.

MOST-RETIRED NUMBERS IN THE NHL (INCLUDING FORMER FRANCHISES)

- **Number 7** – Retired by Boston, Montreal, New York Rangers, Washington Capitals, Detroit Red Wings, Buffalo Sabres, Dallas Stars, Philadelphia Flyers, Edmonton Oilers

- **Number 9** – Boston Bruins, New York Islanders, Detroit Red Wings, Hartford Whalers, Chicago Blackhawks, Calgary Flames, Montreal Canadiens

- **Number 1** – New York Rangers, Philadelphia Flyers, Montreal Canadiens, Detroit Red Wings, Chicago Blackhawks

- **Number 2** – Montreal Canadiens, Buffalo Sabres, St. Louis Blues, Hartford Whalers, Boston Bruins

- **Number 3** – Quebec Nordiques, New Jersey Devils, St. Louis Blues, Boston Bruins, Edmonton Oilers

- **Number 5** – Toronto Maple Leafs, Boston Bruins, Montreal Canadiens, Washington Capitals, New York Islanders

- **Number 16** – Montreal Canadiens, Philadelphia Flyers, Los Angeles Kings, Buffalo Sabres, St. Louis Blues

- **Number 4** – Montreal Canadiens, Philadelphia Flyers, Boston Bruins, New Jersey Devils

* Carolina does not include Whalers' retired numbers. Dallas does honour retired Minnesota numbers. And, although the Leafs no longer retire numbers, those mentioned have actually been retired by the team.

NHL TEAMS
WITH THE MOST RETIRED NUMBERS

11	Montreal Canadiens	1, 2, 4, 5, 7, 9, 10, 12, 16, 18 and 29
10	Boston Bruins	2, 3, 4, 5, 7, 8, 9, 15, 24 and 77
8	Detroit Red Wings	1, 6, 7, 9, 10, 12, 16 and 19
6	Buffalo Sabres	2, 7, 11, 14, 16 and 18
	Edmonton Oilers	3, 7, 11, 17, 31 and 99
	St. Louis Blues	2, 3, 8, 11, 16 and 24
	New York Islanders	5, 9, 19, 22, 23 and 31
5	Chicago Blackhawks	1, 9, 18, 21 and 35
	Los Angeles Kings	16, 18, 20, 30 and 99

NOTE: Technically, every team in the league has retired the number "99." Wayne Gretzky's old number was retired, league-wide, by Commissioner Gary Bettman following The Great One's final game.

TOP-SELLING NHL PLAYER JERSEYS

✓ Peter Forsberg

✓ Sidney Crosby

✓ Jaromir Jagr

✓ Patrick Elias

✓ Mark Messier

✓ Wayne Gretzky

✓ Martin Brodeur

✓ Eric Desjardins

✓ Bobby Orr

✓ Mario Lemieux

*source: SportsOneSource, 2006

TOP-SELLING NHL TEAM JERSEYS

✓ Pittsburgh Penguins (home)

✓ Detroit Red Wings (home)

✓ Buffalo Sabres (home)

✓ Toronto Maple Leafs (home)

✓ Boston Bruins (home)

✓ Montreal Canadiens (home)

✓ Calgary Flames (home, alternate jersey)

✓ Edmonton Oilers (home)

✓ Nashville Predators (road)

✓ Atlanta Thrashers (home)

*source: IceJerseys.com

MOST EXPENSIVE PLACES TO SEE AN NHL GAME

This is based on the cost of four average-priced seats, four small soft drinks, two small beers, four hot dogs, two programs, parking and two caps — in other words, what an average family might spend to go to a game.

Montreal

Boston

New Jersey

Vancouver

Philadelphia

Minnesota

New York (Rangers)

Edmonton

Calgary

Los Angeles

...AND THE LEAST EXPENSIVE

Phoenix

Buffalo

St. Louis

Anaheim

Pittsburgh

Carolina

San Jose

Chicago

Washington

Dallas

* Source: Teammarketingreport.com

TEN LARGEST SEATING CAPACITIES IN THE NHL ... AND THE TEN SMALLEST

TEN LARGEST	TEN SMALLEST
Montreal – 21,273	New York Islanders – 16,234
Chicago – 20,500	Edmonton – 16,839
Detroit – 20,066	Pittsburgh – 16,940
Tampa Bay – 19,758	Nashville – 17,113
Philadelphia – 19,523	Anaheim – 17,174
Calgary – 19,289	San Jose – 17,496
Florida – 19,250	Boston – 17,565
Ottawa – 19,153	Phoenix – 17,799
New Jersey – 19,040	Colorado – 18,007
St. Louis – 19,022	Minnesota – 18,064

HISTORY

Great old buildings, expansion teams that just didn't make it and a few championship trophies I'll bet you'd never heard of.

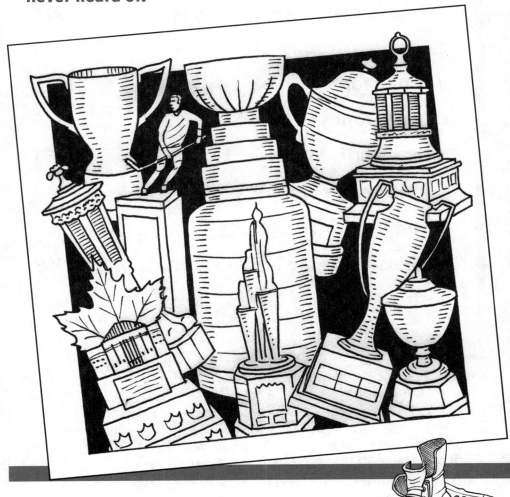

OLDEST NHL AWARDS

Stanley Cup	1893*
Hart Trophy	1923†
Prince of Wales Trophy	1924
Lady Byng Trophy	1924‡
Vezina Trophy	1926
Calder Trophy	1936
James Norris Memorial Trophy	1953
Conn Smythe Trophy	1964
Lester Patrick Trophy	1966
Bill Masterton Memorial Trophy	1968
Lester B. Pearson Award	1970–71

* First awarded in 1893 to the Montreal Amateur Athletic Association. It is the oldest trophy competed for by professional athletes in North America.

† The original Hart Trophy was donated to the NHL in 1923 by Dr. David A. Hart, father of former Montreal Canadiens manager-coach Cecil Hart. In 1960, it was retired to the Hockey Hall of Fame and replaced by the present one.

‡ After Frank Boucher of the New York Rangers won the trophy seven times, he was allowed to keep it. A new one was presented in 1939. After Lady Byng's death in 1949, the NHL presented the one we've come to know today.

CURRENT NHL TEAMS THAT HAVE WON STANLEY CUPS

Montreal Canadiens* – **23**	New Jersey Devils – **3**
Toronto Maple Leafs – **13**	Philadelphia Flyers – **2**
Detroit Red Wings – **10**	Pittsburgh Penguins – **2**
Boston Bruins – **5**	Colorado Avalanche – **2**
Edmonton Oilers – **5**	Dallas Stars – **1**
New York Rangers – **4**	Calgary Flames – **1**
New York Islanders – **4**	Tampa Bay Lightning – **1**
Chicago Blackhawks – **3**	Carolina Hurricanes – **1**
	Anaheim Ducks – **1**

* Some argue that the Canadiens have won the Cup 24 times, but the championship in 1916 was prior to the formation of the NHL — so the official league total is 23.

The 1927 Stanley Cup

WE WERE THE CHAMPIONS

It's been a long wait for some teams and their fans. Below is the last time some teams have been able to hoist the Cup.

✓	Chicago Blackhawks	1960–61
✓	Toronto Maple Leafs	1966–67
✓	Boston Bruins	1971–72
✓	Philadelphia Flyers	1974–75
✓	New York Islanders	1982–83
✓	Calgary Flames	1988–89

MOST CONSECUTIVE YEARS IN THE PLAYOFFS

29 – Boston Bruins	1968 — 1996
28 – Chicago Blackhawks	1970 — 1997
25 – St. Louis Blues	1980 — 2004
24 – Montreal Canadiens	1971 — 1994
20 – Detroit Red Wings	1939 — 1958
17 – Philadelphia Flyers	1973 — 1989
16 – Atlanta / Calgary Flames	1976 — 1991
15 – Toronto Maple Leafs	1931 — 1946
14 – Washington Capitals	1983 — 1996
14 – New York Islanders	1975 — 1988

10 The price, in guineas, that the Stanley Cup was purchased for in 1892. At the time it would have been about $50 Canadian.

OLDEST ARENAS IN THE NHL

Mellon Arena
Home of the Pittsburgh Penguins   **1961**

Madison Square Garden
Home of the New York Rangers   **1968**

Nassau Veterans Memorial Coliseum
Home of the New York Islanders   **1972**

Rexall Place
Home of the Edmonton Oilers   **1974**

Joe Louis Arena
Home of the Detroit Red Wings   **1979**

SOME GREAT BUILDINGS NO LONGER IN THE NHL

Maple Leaf Gardens

Along with the Montreal Forum, a temple of hockey to most Canadians. It stands on the corner of Carlton Street and Church Street, and was home to the Toronto Maple Leafs from 1931 to 1999.

The Montreal Forum

The Forum was home to the Montreal Canadiens from 1924 to 1996, and sat at the corner of Atwater Avenue and St. Catherine Street. The standing room just above the lower level . . . the smell of hot dogs . . . the Stanley Cup banners — the building was a monument to hockey and tradition.

Chicago Stadium

Home to the Blackhawks from 1929 to 1994, Chicago Stadium was lovingly referred to as "The Madhouse on Madison Street." The most amazing feature of the building was a massive pipe organ that was built right into the wall. When the organ was played loudly, the entire building shook.

Boston Garden

This is where the Bruins played from 1928 until 1995. It was a quirky old building with loads of character. The ice surface was smaller than normal, the visitors' dressing room was a closet, and there was no air conditioning. Come to think of it, it's just as well they closed the place down.

FAILED NHL TEAMS

Not every idea is a good one . . .

Quebec Bulldogs (1919–20)

They lasted only one season in the NHL, although there was another version of this franchise kicking around before the NHL was formed that was actually very successful (they won the Stanley Cup in 1912 and 1913). This version of the team lasted one season, when the team only won 4 out of 24 games. They were moved to Hamilton, Ontario, at the end of the season.

Hamilton Tigers (1920–1926)

After the Quebec Bulldogs relocated to Hamilton, the team continued to play horribly. Their luck seemed to turn around though when, in 1924–25, they finished first in the league. But after a salary dispute, the team refused to take to the ice for the finals. League president Frank Calder fined and suspended them, awarding the league title to the Canadiens. This was the end for the NHL in Hamilton. But they got their raise — after a New York businessman bought the team and moved them to the Big Apple.

Philadelphia Quakers (1930–1931)

Many years before the Philadelphia Flyers were even an idea, the Quakers played their first NHL game in the City of Brotherly Love. The Quakers were moved to Philadelphia from Pittsburgh (where they were the Pirates). The team was awful. They went 4–36–4 (wins, losses and ties) in their one and only active season in the league.

Oakland/California Golden Seals (1967 – 1976)

This woeful franchise struggled along for nine seasons, going through several owners, general managers, coaches and players. They only made the playoffs twice, and never won a series. Their most notable contribution to hockey was wearing white skates for the 1970–1971 season. The franchise was moved to Cleveland in 1976.

Cleveland Barons (1976 – 1978)

The dark cloud hanging over the California Seals followed them to Cleveland. The Barons played in an 18,544-seat arena located far outside the city in the middle of farming country — not exactly an easy place for the people of Cleveland to get to. The team missed the playoffs both seasons and was merged with the Minnesota North Stars after the 1977–78 season.

Kansas City Scouts (1974 – 1976)

In 1974 hockey in Kansas City, Missouri, seemed like a great idea to the people running the NHL. Apparently no one asked the people who lived in Kansas City how they felt about getting an NHL team. After two seasons of playing in front of empty seats, the Scouts were moved to Denver, Colorado.

NHL COMMISSIONERS AND LEAGUE

Frank Calder

The first, and greatest, NHL leader. Calder was the league president from its inception in 1917 until his death in 1943. He saw the league through two global wars and the Great Depression of the 1930s. The award for NHL Rookie of the Year bears his name.

"Red" Dutton

Dutton agreed to take over the presidency after the sudden death of Calder. He held the position until 1946 when he left the league to return to private business.

Clarence Campbell

Campbell is credited with ushering in the modern era of the NHL. Under his leadership, from 1946 to 1977, the league expanded from 6 to 18 teams. The NHL Western Conference Champion is presented with the Clarence Campbell Bowl.

13 The time, in years, it takes to fill one ring of the Stanley Cup

PRESIDENTS

John Ziegler

From 1977 until 1992, Ziegler guided the NHL through expansion, labour issues with the NHLPA and the growth of the sport in the U.S. He was the first American-born NHL president.

Gil Stein

His brief reign lasted one season, from 1992–1993, during which he infamously arranged his own nomination to be inducted into the Hockey Hall of Fame. After being discovered, Stein withdrew the nomination.

Gary Bettman

A former National Basketball Association executive, Bettman has run the NHL since 1993. He is the first leader to use the term "commissioner" rather than "president." Bettman is responsible for the expansion of the league to many non-traditional hockey markets (Dallas, Florida, Carolina) and also the participation of NHL players in the Winter Olympics.

HOCKEY CHAMPIONSHIP TROPHIES

Allan Cup

This trophy was first presented in 1908 to the Canadian amateur hockey champion. Competition qualifications have changed over the years, but presently the trophy goes to the Canadian Senior AAA teams.

Calder Cup

This was first presented in 1937. It is the championship trophy for the American Hockey League.

Memorial Cup

This beautiful trophy was first presented in 1919 and was named to commemorate the thousands of Canadian men and women who were killed during the First World War. It is presented to the Canadian Hockey League (junior hockey) champion.

Spengler Cup

This trophy goes to the winner of the oldest club team tournament in Europe, and is one of the oldest in the world. The tournament is played in Davos, Switzerland, each December.

Abby Hoffman Cup

A fairly new trophy, this Cup was first presented in 1983 to the top provincial women's hockey team in Canada. The trophy is named after Abby Hoffman, a pioneer in women's hockey.

World Hockey Championship

There have been several versions of a trophy for the annual IIHF World Hockey Championship. The most recent was unveiled in 2001 and weighs in at a hefty 10 kilograms.

University Cup

Presented to the top team in Canadian university hockey, it's been around since 1963.

NCAA Championship Trophy

Presented to the winner of the Frozen Four tournament (among the top four teams in U.S. Division I hockey) held each April. The title goes back to 1948.

Continental Cup

This trophy goes to the winner of a season-long tournament held among 48 of the top club teams in Europe. It was first presented in 1998 and was a continuation of the IIHF European Champions Cup tournament.

Kelly Cup

The championship trophy for the East Coast Hockey League has been presented since 1997.

BEEN THERE, DONE THAT

The NHL was founded in 1917–18. Here are some of the oldest franchises in their original cities:

ORIGINAL SIX ERA

1917–18	Montreal Canadiens
	Toronto Maple Leafs
1933–34	Ottawa Senators*
1924–25	Boston Bruins†
1926–27	Chicago Blackhawks
	Detroit Red Wings
	New York Rangers

MODERN ERA

1967–68	Los Angeles Kings
	Philadelphia Flyers
	Pittsburgh Penguins
	St. Louis Blues
1970–71	Buffalo Sabres
	Vancouver Canucks
1972–73	New York Islanders
1974–75	Washington Capitals
1979–80	Edmonton Oilers‡
1991–92	San Jose Sharks

* Franchise was transferred to St. Louis after the 1933–34 season. The modern version of the Sens didn't show up until 1992–93.
† The NHL's first American team.
‡ Came into the NHL after the demise of the World Hockey Association.

PEOPLE

Sports is all about the characters and their accomplishments — can you believe Roger Neilson coached 8 different NHL teams?

GREAT MUSTACHIOED PLAYERS

━━━ Lanny McDonald

Great career! Great walrus mustache! McDonald has the all-time finest facial hair in hockey. He scored 500 career goals, had 506 assists and was one of the greatest right wingers of his era.

Lanny McDonald

Derek "Turk" Sanderson

Played in the NHL from 1967 until 1978
Sanderson was one of the most flamboyant players ever. He'd wear his big, black, bushy mustache while sporting a long fur coat and driving a silver Rolls Royce. He was the NHL rookie of the year in 1968, and part of two Stanley Cup Championships with Boston.

Bob Nystrom

New York Islanders' rough-and-tumble right winger
Nystrom played 900 games in the NHL from 1972 until 1986. His dark blond mustache curled around the corners of his mouth.

Mel Bridgman

Played mainly with Philadelphia and New Jersey from 1975 to 1989
He sported a black cookie-duster for most of his career.

Dan Bain

One of Canada's greatest athletes
Bain was voted "Canada's Athlete" of the last half of the 19th century. A dark handlebar mustache, a fashion of the day, made its home just above his top lip.

MOST STANLEY CUP CHAMPIONSHIPS AS A PLAYER

11 Henri Richard	**6** Tom Johnson
10 Jean Beliveau	Dick Duff
Yvan Cournoyer	Doug Harvey
9 Claude Provost	Larry Hillman
8 Maurice "The Rocket" Richard	Jacques Laperriere
Red Kelly	Ralph Backstrom
Jacques Lemaire	Jacques Plante
Serge Savard	Dickie Moore
7 Jean-Guy Talbot	Frank Mahovlich
	Ken Dryden
	Guy Lapointe
	Mark Messier
	Kevin Lowe

GRETZKY'S FAVOURITE TEAMS

The Great One piled on the points against these teams.

Vancouver Canucks	**239**
Calgary Flames / Atlanta Flames	**230**
Phoenix Coyotes / Winnipeg Jets	**230**
Los Angeles Kings	**179**
Toronto Maple Leafs	**150**
Detroit Red Wings	**145**
Colorado Avalanche / Quebec Nordiques	**132**
Pittsburgh Penguins	**124**
New Jersey Devils / Colorado Rockies	**123**
Dallas Stars / Minnesota North Stars	**116**
Carolina Hurricanes / Hartford Whalers	**109**
St. Louis Blues	**107**

BRILLIANT SCOUTING

There are many reasons why good players slip through the cracks and don't get drafted until the later rounds — injuries, bad scouting, good scouting. Here are a few late-round success stories:

▬ Dominik Hasek   1990–91

The finest goaltender of his era; has won it all — the Vezina Trophy, Hart Trophy, Lester B. Pearson Award and William Jennings Trophy

In 1983, while he was playing in his native Czechoslovakia, he was a mystery to most NHL scouts. For that reason, he was the 207th overall pick by Chicago in the 1983 Entry Draft.

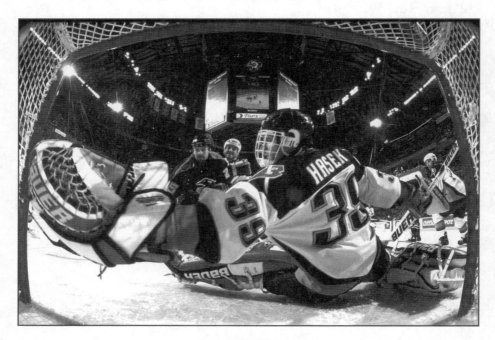

▬▬ Dino Ciccarelli   1980–81 to 1998–99

Played 1,232 games in the NHL with the Minnesota North Stars, Washington Capitals, Detroit Red Wings, Tampa Bay Lightning and Florida Panthers; finished with 1,200 career points

Which brilliant team drafted him? None! Ciccarelli suffered a badly broken leg in junior hockey during his draft year, and no team bothered picking him up. Minnesota signed him as a free agent a few months after the draft.

▬▬ Theoren Fleury   1988–89 to 2002–03

Played 1,084 games in the NHL with Calgary, the New York Rangers and Chicago; averaged better than a point per game, finishing with 1,088 points

He's the all-time Calgary Flames points leader . . . but he wasn't picked until the Flames took him 166th overall in the 1987 draft. At 1.68 m and 75 kg (5'6" and 165 lbs) — many said that was being generous — most scouts thought Theo was too small for the NHL. ●

By the numbers

171 Goals given up by the Montreal Canadiens during their record-setting eight-loss season in 1976–77

FIRST-ROUND FLOPS

It's tough for teams: drafting a junior player when he's 18 years old and hoping he'll be a solid NHL player one day. It's a gamble, and sometimes you win, sometimes you lose. But remember: hindsight is always 20/20!

Bjorn Johansson

Fifth overall pick of the California Golden Seals, 1976 NHL Entry Draft

The Swedish defenseman was the first European-born player to be taken in the first round of the draft. He only played 15 games in the NHL before heading home.

Doug Wickenheiser

First overall pick of the Montreal Canadiens, 1980 NHL Entry Draft

Doug played 551 games in the NHL over 10 seasons. But, for a first overall pick, his total of 276 points wasn't very impressive.

Brian Lawton

First overall pick of the Minnesota North Stars, 1983 NHL Entry Draft

He was the first U.S. high school player ever to be drafted number one overall. He never met expectations, managing only 112 goals in nine seasons.

Benoit Larose

Fifth overall pick of the Detroit Red Wings, 1993 NHL Entry Draft

He didn't play a single second in the NHL.

Jason Bonsignore

Fourth overall pick of the Edmonton Oilers, 1994 NHL Entry Draft

At 1.93 m, 100 kg (6'4", 220 lbs) he was expected to be a force in the NHL. He wasn't. Jason never played a full season in the NHL and finished his career playing in Europe.

COACHES WITH THE MOST WINS (NHL)

🏒 Scotty Bowman	**1,244**
🏒 Al Arbour	**781**
🏒 Dick Irvin Sr.	**692**
🏒 Pat Quinn	**657**
🏒 Bryan Murray	**613**
🏒 Mike Keenan	**584**
🏒 Billy Reay	**542**
🏒 Glen Sather	**502**
🏒 Pat Burns	**501**
🏒 Toe Blake	**500**

MOST STANLEY CUP CHAMPIONSHIPS
FOR A COACH

9	Scotty Bowman	3	Jack Adams
8	Toe Blake		Pete Green
5	Hap Day		Tommy Ivan
4	Al Arbour	2	Tommy Gorman
	Punch Imlach		Cecil Hart
	Glen Sather		Lester Patrick
	Dick Irvin Sr.		Claude Ruel
			Fred Shero

By the numbers 18277 349-2 562

2,141 NHL games coached by Scotty Bowman, the coach who has the most wins in NHL history

MOST TEAMS COACHED

8	Roger Neilson	**4**	Sid Abel
	Mike Keenan		Bob Berry
5	Scotty Bowman		Georges Boucher
	Rick Bowness		Herb Brooks
	Jacques Demers		Pat Burns
	Bryan Murray		Eddie Gerard
			John Muckler
			Pierre Page
			Pat Quinn
			Jim Schoenfeld
			Brian Sutter
			Johnny Wilson

MOST TEAMS PLAYED FOR IN AN NHL CAREER

12	Mike Sillinger	1990–2006
10	Michel Petit	1982–1998
	J. J. Daigneault	1984–2001
9	Bobby Dollas	1983–2001
	Kevin Miller	1988–2004
	Brent Ashton	1979–1993
	Jim Cummins	1991–2004
	Tony Hrkac	1986–2003
	Bryan Marchment	1988–2006
	Jim McKenzie	1989–2004
	Grant Ledyard	1984–2002
	Reid Simpson	1991–2004
	Paul Coffey	1980–2001
	Jim Dowd	1991–2006

PLACES GRETZKY SCORED THE MOST GOALS

Wayne is the greatest goal-scorer in the history of the game, but there were a few places where he really went to town — his home rinks for a start.

Rexall Place, Edmonton	**327 goals**
Great Western Forum, Los Angeles	**171 goals**
Madison Square Garden, New York City	**46 goals**
Winnipeg Arena, Winnipeg	**38 goals**
Pacific Coliseum, Vancouver	**30 goals**
Maple Leaf Gardens, Toronto	**30 goals**
Pengrowth Saddledome, Calgary	**21 goals**
Civic Arena, Pittsburgh	**21 goals**
St. Louis Arena, St. Louis	**16 goals**
Nassau Coliseum, Long Island	**16 goals**

PEOPLE

GRETZKY'S TOP TEN SEASONS

Take a look at The Great One's ten best seasons — and consider that nearly half of them included over 200 points.

1985–86	**52** goals, **163** assists, **215** points
1981–82	**92** goals, **120** assists, **212** points*
1984–85	**73** goals, **135** assists, **208** points
1983–84	**87** goals, **118** assists, **205** points
1982–83	**71** goals, **125** assists, **196** points
1986–87	**62** goals, **121** assists, **183** points
1988–89	**54** goals, **114** assists, **168** points†
1980–81	**55** goals, **109** assists, **164** points
1990–91	**41** goals, **122** assists, **163** points
1987–88	**40** goals, **109** assists, **149** points

* Interestingly, in Gretzky's two best individual seasons, the Oilers did not win the Stanley Cup.
† Finished second to Mario Lemieux and his 199 points

BIG NIGHTS FOR THE GREAT ONE

First NHL Game

This was on October 10, 1979, against the Chicago Black Hawks. He picked up an assist on Kevin Lowe's first-period goal.

First NHL Goal

Gretzky's first goal came 3 games into his first season, October 14, 1979, against the Vancouver Canucks and goalie Glen Hanlon.

50 Goals in 39 Games

On December 30, 1981, Gretzky scored 5 goals in Edmonton against the Philadelphia Flyers and reached the 50-goal mark in an NHL-record 39 games.

Single Season Goal Record

On February 24, 1982, Gretzky scored his 77th goal of the season to break the record held by Phil Esposito for most goals in a season. Gretzky went on to score a record 92 goals.

First Stanley Cup

Gretzky had to wait until his fifth NHL season to hoist the Cup over his head. The date was May 19, 1984, and the Oilers defeated the New York Islanders in 5 games in the final.

Canada Cup

The Great One has a distinguished career with Team Canada that continues to this day as a general manager and advisor. On September 15, 1987, he set up Mario Lemieux to score the winning goal in the championship game against the USSR. The goal came with 1:26 remaining, and Canada won 6–5.

Last Cup

May 26, 1988 was not only the date of his fourth, and final, Stanley Cup title — but also his final game with the Edmonton Oilers.

Traded to Los Angeles

On August 9, 1988, a deal shocked Canada and the rest of the hockey world — Gretzky was traded to the Los Angeles Kings in a deal orchestrated by then Edmonton owner Peter Pocklington.

Becomes All-Time Points Leader

As fate would have it, Gretzky was with the Kings playing a game in Edmonton on October 15, 1989. This was the night Gretzky scored in the final minute for career-point 1,851 to become the all-time NHL regular season points leader, passing his boyhood hero, "Mr. Hockey," Gordie Howe. For good measure, he also scored the winner for the Kings in overtime.

Last Game

Gretzky's last game was at Madison Square Garden in New York City, against the Pittsburgh Penguins on April 18, 1999. Fittingly, as he'd picked up one assist in his first NHL game, Gretzky assisted on the Rangers' only goal in his final NHL game.

TOP PLAY-BY-PLAY ANNOUNCERS

Danny Gallivan

The finest English-speaking ice hockey play-by-play man ever — Danny called over 1,800 Montreal Canadiens games over a 32-year career in the booth. Classic phrases include "Savardian spin-a-rama" for a spin move used by Montreal defenseman Serge Savard and "[He] fires that leg out in rapier-like fashion" for a great kick save by a goalie.

Dan Kelly

The legendary voice of the St. Louis Blues for over 20 years — Dan was well-known to hockey fans all over North America because of his work on network television in Canada and the U.S.

René Lecavalier

As famous to French-Canadians as his English counterpart Danny Gallivan — René called games on the *Le Soiree de hockey* for over 30 years and was known for his spectacular and elegant use of the language.

Pierre Houde

The number one voice of hockey in French Canada today — Houde is known for his knowledge and fairness as well as his sense of humour with on-air partner Yvon Pedneault.

Bob Cole

The main play-by-play voice of *Hockey Night in Canada* for over 30 years — Bob could make two guys fishing sound exciting, and his ability to anticipate a big play is second to none.

Foster Hewitt

Foster Hewitt

The father of hockey play-by-play — He may not have been the best, but he was the first. He coined the phrase "He shoots, he scores!"

Bill Hewitt

Son of Foster Hewitt — He learned from the master, calling part of a game on the radio when he was only 8 years old. He was the voice of the Toronto Maple Leafs on television for 20 years.

Mike "Doc" Emrick

Voice of NHL FaceOff PlayStation games — He's also called NHL play-by-play, on radio and television, in the U.S. for over 25 years.

Jim Robson

Broadcast over 2,000 games on radio and television (mainly for the Vancouver Canucks) — Jim also appeared on *Hockey Night in Canada* for 15 years. His signature mid-game greeting was always to "hospital patients and shut-ins and people who can't get out to hockey games."

Mike Lange

The long-time voice of the Pittsburgh Penguins — Known to fans all over the hockey world for his amazingly colourful goal calls, including: "Heeeeee shoots and scores!"

YOU PLAYED HOW MANY GAMES?

Players who played just one game in the NHL

Don Cherry	Boston Bruins, 1955
Ken Brown	Chicago Black Hawks, 1970–71
Dean Morton	Detroit Red Wings, 1989–90
Bill Armstrong	Philadelphia Flyers, 1990–91
Sebastien Centomo	Toronto Maple Leafs, 2001–02
Pauli Jaks	Los Angeles Kings, 1994–95
Jason Herter	New York Islanders, 1995–96
Luke Sellars	Atlanta Thrashers, 2001–02
Travis Scott	Los Angeles Kings, 2000–01
Brandy Semchuk	Los Angeles Kings, 1992–93

MIKE LANGE'S BEST GOAL CALLS

The legendary voice of the Pittsburgh Penguins has a way with words.

- "Buy Sam a drink and get his dog one too."

- "Scratch my back with a hacksaw."

- "He beat him like a rented mule!"

- "Michael, Michael motorcycle."

- "Well, I'll be cow-kicked."

- "He's smiling like a butcher's dog."

- "Let's go hunt a moose on a Harley."

- "Get in the fast lane grandma, the bingo game is ready to roll."

- "Great balls of fire!"

GRETZKY'S FAVOURITE HELPERS

Players who assisted on the most regular season goals scored by The Great One

Jari Kurri	**196**
Paul Coffey	**116**
Mark Messier	**68**
Glenn Anderson	**63**
Luc Robitaille	**46**
Mike Krushelnyski	**40**
Kevin Lowe	**37**
Esa Tikkanen	**33**

HAVEN'T I SEEN YOU SOMEWHERE BEFORE?

Players who laced 'em up the most times with Gretzky

Jari Kurri	**858** games
Mark Messier	**698** games
Charlie Huddy	**664** games
Kevin Lowe	**661** games
Dave Hunter	**613** games
Glenn Anderson	**591** games
Lee Fogolin Jr.	**579** games
Marty McSorley	**556** games
Paul Coffey	**546** games
Luc Robitaille	**491** games

TEN THINGS YOU MIGHT NOT KNOW

1. Bucko McDonald, a former NHL defenseman, was one of Bobby Orr's first coaches when he played minor hockey in Parry Sound, Ontario.

2. The Boston Bruins scout who signed Bobby, at the age of 12, was Wren Blair.

3. Bobby was 14 years old in his first season of junior hockey.

4. In his first season of junior hockey, with the Oshawa Generals, Bobby commuted from his home in Parry Sound. As a result, he didn't practise once with the team that season.

5. He was 1.68 m and 61 kg in his rookie year with the Generals.

6. Bobby signed the first $1,000,000 deal in hockey in 1971 — five years at $200,000 per season.

7. Bobby's first number with the Bruins wasn't the legendary "4" — he was given "27" at his first training camp.

ABOUT BOBBY ORR

8. In his first NHL All-Star Game, Bobby wore the number "5" instead of his usual "4" because that number belonged to veteran Jean Beliveau.

9. According to Bobby's father, Doug, when Bobby started skating at the age of four "he really ran around on his ankles a lot." He went on to become one of the greatest skaters in the history of the game.

10. Bobby was awarded the Order of Canada — the nation's highest civil honour — in 1979.

Bobby Orr

PLAYERS WHO SCORED IN THEIR ONLY GAME

■ Dean Morton

Scored in a game for Detroit during the 1989–90 season before being sent back down to the minors

■ Brad Fast

Played in a late-season game for Carolina in 2003–04 and scored against Florida in a 6–6 tie

■ Rolly Huard

Played one game as an emergency injury replacement for the Toronto Maple Leafs on December 14, 1930, and managed to score

GRETZKY'S FAVOURITE GOALIES

Not sure they felt quite the same about Wayne . . .

Richard Brodeur	**29** goals scored against
Mike Liut	**23** goals scored against
Don Beaupre	**21** goals scored against
Kirk McLean	**21** goals scored against
Greg Millen	**21** goals scored against
Don Edwards	**18** goals scored against
Bill Ranford	**18** goals scored against
Reggie Lemelin	**17** goals scored against
Mario Lessard	**17** goals scored against
Mike Vernon	**17** goals scored against

TEN PLAYERS WHO SPENT MOST OF THEIR

━━━ Willie Marshall

Played 1,205 games in the American Hockey League — the all-time leader in games played in that league; also played 33 games with the Toronto Maple Leafs

━━━ Fred Glover

Played 1,201 games in the AHL; also played 92 NHL games and got his name on the Stanley Cup in 1952 with Detroit

━━━ Harry Pidhirny

Played 1,071 games in the AHL; 2 NHL games with Boston

━━━ Mike Nykoluk

Played 1,069 AHL games and 32 games with the Toronto Maple Leafs; later coached the Leafs

━━━ Jody Gage

Played 1,038 AHL games and another 68 in the NHL

CAREER IN THE MINORS

Rob Murray

Played 1,018 games in the AHL as well as 107 in the NHL

Bill Needham

Played the most games in the minors — 981 games in the AHL — without playing a single minute in the NHL

Ken Gernander

Played 973 games in the AHL and another 10 in the NHL

Jim Bartlett

Played 955 AHL games and another 191 games in the NHL

Jimmy Anderson

Played 943 games in the AHL and another 7 with the Los Angeles Kings

TEN THINGS YOU MIGHT NOT KNOW ABOUT

1. Wayne first skated in 1963, at the age of 2 years and 10 months near his grandparents' farm near the Nith River near Brantford, Ontario.

2. Wayne called the backyard rink his father built for him "Wally Coliseum" — after his father, Walter Gretzky.

3. In Wayne's first season with his first minor hockey team he scored a grand total of one goal.

4. The first hockey trophy Wayne ever won was in 1969 for being "The Most Improved Novice All-Star."

5. Wayne's first number was "3."

6. Wayne's first goals in Junior B, Junior A, the WHA and the NHL were all scored on backhand shots.

7. Wayne first met hockey legend Gordie Howe at a banquet in Brantford, Ontario, in 1972. There is a famous picture of the 44-year-old Howe playfully hooking 11-year-old Gretzky around the neck with a hockey stick.

8. During the 1971–72 season, Wayne scored 378 goals in 82 games with the Nadrofsky Steelers Novice All Stars.

WAYNE GRETZKY

9. The number "99" became Wayne's when he played for the Soo Greyhounds in the Ontario Hockey League. He wanted "9," but a veteran player already had it. He tried "19" and "14" before coach Muzz MacPherson convinced him to wear "99."

10. Hard to believe, but no fans in the NHL booed Gretzky more than fans at Maple Leaf Gardens in Toronto. He was in good company, however; they used to boo Bobby Orr, too.

Wayne Gretzky in the 1978 Junior All-Star Game

TEN THINGS YOU MIGHT NOT KNOW ABOUT MARIO LEMIEUX

1. Mario was born on the same day as the great Patrick Roy — October 5, 1965.

2. In his final regular season game in junior hockey, with the Laval Voisins, Mario scored 6 goals and assisted on 6.

3. He scored a goal on his first shot of his first shift in his first game in the NHL.

4. His first NHL fight (there weren't many afterward) was against Gary Lupul of the Vancouver Canucks.

5. Mario's older brother, Alain, played parts of six seasons in the NHL.

6. Scotty Bowman, the greatest coach in NHL history, called Mario "the most complete player I've ever seen."

7. Mario is an avid wine collector.

8. When Sidney Crosby was a rookie, he lived with Mario and his family in Pittsburgh.

9. Mario and his wife, Nathalie, met when he was 16 and she was 15.

10. Mario is a very good golfer.

AROUND THE WORLD

It's a big world out there — and a lot of it loves hockey.

INTERNATIONAL ICE HOCKEY FEDERATION (IIHF)
MEMBER COUNTRIES WITH THE MOST INDOOR ICE RINKS

Canada	**3,000***
United States	**1,800**
Sweden	**307**
Finland	**220**
Germany	**158**
Czech Republic	**152**
Russia	**142**
Japan	**130**
France	**128**
Switzerland	**70**

* There are another 11,000 outdoor rinks in Canada — more than
  10 times as many as the rest of the world combined!

IIHF COUNTRIES WHERE HOCKEY IS STILL GROWING

These are all countries that are official members of the IIHF, but where ice hockey is still growing.

🏒 **Portugal**

Only 43 registered players in the entire country and 1 ice rink

🏒 **Ireland**

Almost double the number of players (75) and double the number of ice rinks (2) as Portugal

🏒 **Andorra**

One lonely ice rink for 83 players

🏒 **Luxembourg**

Three rinks for 320 players

🏒 **Greece**

Only 1 rink and 326 players looking for a game

By the numbers

268 Distance, one way in kilometres, between Parry Sound, Ontario, where Bobby Orr lived during his rookie season in the OHL, and Oshawa, Ontario, where he played

PLACES WHERE HOCKEY IS BIGGER THAN YOU THINK

✓ **Austria**

Over 31,000 players and 55 ice rinks in a country better known for skiing.

✓ **Japan**

Close to 200 ice rinks for almost 20,000 players.

✓ **Great Britain**

A surprising 8,401 registered players as well as a decent professional league.

✓ **The Netherlands**

Soccer is king, but nearly 3,500 try to get in a game once or twice a week.

✓ **North Korea**

Nearly 3,000 people play on mainly outdoor rinks.

✓ **Poland**

Over 2,000 registered players, but only 28 ice rinks in the country.

✓ **Mexico**

A tough one to figure out — only 9 ice rinks in the entire country, but over 1,100 players.

IIHF COUNTRIES WITH THE MOST REGISTERED PLAYERS

Canada	552,040
United States	453,299
Czech Republic	87,130
Russia	77,202
Sweden	65,739

1961 The year the Hockey Hall of Fame opened in Toronto

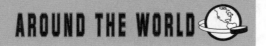
COUNTRIES WITH THE MOST FEMALE REGISTERED PLAYERS

Canada	**66,000**
United States	**53,030**
Sweden	**3,398**
France	**2,862**
Finland	**2,467**

1952 The year *Hockey Night in Canada* debuted

TOP HOCKEY-PLAYER
PRODUCING COUNTRIES

- Canada

- United States of America

- Soviet Union / Commonwealth of Independent States / Russia

- Sweden

- Czechoslovakia / Czech Republic / Slovakia

- Finland

- Switzerland

- Germany

- Norway

- Denmark

BIG INTERNATIONAL HOCKEY EVENTS

1 **1972 Summit Series** – The first and most famous international hockey tournament — eight games between a group of Canadian-born NHL stars and the greatest Soviet hockey players of the time. Canada won the deciding game on Paul Henderson's goal with 34 seconds to play.

2 **1974 Summit Series** – The lesser-known but highly entertaining series between the Soviet stars and a group of Canadian-born players from the World Hockey Association. Canada didn't fare as well in this 8-game series, winning only 2, while losing 4 and tying 2.

3 **1976 Canada Cup** – The forerunner to the present-day World Cup of Hockey, this tournament was the first to feature all of the best players in the NHL playing for their respective countries. Canada won the first one by defeating Czechoslovakia in the final. Canada Cup tournaments were also held in 1981, 1984, 1987 and 1991.

4 **Super Series** – The first time club teams from the Soviet Union and Czechoslovakia played NHL teams during the middle of the season. The first of several series was played in 1975–76. The most memorable game was a classic matchup between the Montreal Canadiens and the Soviet Red Army on New Year's Eve in 1975, when the two clubs battled to a 3–3 tie.

5 **Challenge Cup** – The Soviets played an NHL All-Star Team in a three game series at Madison Square Garden in New York during the 1979 All-Star break. The Soviets won the series.

6 **Rendez-Vous** – A two-game series played in Quebec City during the 1987 All-Star break between the Soviet National Team and a group of NHL All-Stars. Each team won one game.

7 **World Cup of Hockey** – Started in 1996 by the NHL, NHLPA and the IIHF, this tournament is a modern version of the Canada Cup, providing an opportunity for the best players from the NHL to play for their respective countries. The first one was held in 1996, followed by another in 2004.

8 **Wayne Gretzky "Lockout Tour"** – During the 1994 labour dispute between the NHL and the NHLPA, Wayne Gretzky put together a group of NHL players and toured Sweden, Finland, Norway and Russia.

9 **Friendship Tours** – During the 1989 and 1990 pre-seasons, the Calgary Flames, Washington Capitals, Montreal Canadiens and Minnesota North Stars toured the Soviet Union and faced four different Soviet club teams.

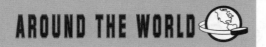
COUNTRIES THAT HAVE WON
THE IIHF WORLD CHAMPIONSHIP THE MOST TIMES

Canada	24
USSR	22
Sweden	8
Czechoslovakia	6
Czech Republic	5
United States	2
Finland	1
Great Britain	
Slovakia	
Russia	

PLAYERS WHO'VE PLAYED THE MOST GAMES FOR THEIR NATIONAL TEAM

Raimo Helminen – Finland	**330**
Udo Kiessling – West Germany	**320**
Jiri Holik – Czechoslovakia	**319**
Alexander Maltsev – USSR	**316**
Sergei Makarov – USSR	**315**
Diemtar Peters – East Germany	
Vyacheslav Fetisov – USSR	**314**
Alexei Kasatonov – USSR	**299**
Dieter Frenzel – East Germany	**296**
Oldrich Machac – Czechoslovakia	**293**

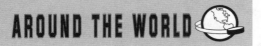
PLAYERS WHO'VE WON THE MOST WORLD CHAMPIONSHIP MEDALS

Do you think the Soviets dominated the World Championship?

Vladislav Tretiak – USSR	**13 medals** – 10 gold, 2 silver, 1 bronze
Alexander Ragulin – USSR	**12 medals** – 10 gold, 1 silver, 1 bronze
Alexander Maltsev – USSR	**12 medals** – 9 gold, 2 silver, 1 bronze
Vladimir Petrov – USSR	**12 medals** – 9 gold, 2 silver, 1 bronze
Boris Mikhailov – USSR	**11 medals** – 8 gold, 2 silver, 1 bronze
Valeri Kharlamov – USSR	**11 medals** – 8 gold, 2 silver, 1 bronze
Vladimir Lutchenko – USSR	**11 medals** – 8 gold, 2 silver, 1 bronze
Valeri Vasiliev – USSR	**11 medals** – 8 gold, 2 silver, 1 bronze
Sergei Makarov – USSR	**11 medals** – 8 gold, 2 silver, 1 bronze
Vatali Davydov – USSR	**10 medals** – 9 gold, 1 silver
Vyacheslav Starshinov – USSR	**10 medals** – 9 gold, 1 bronze
Vyacheslav Fetisov – USSR	**10 medals** – 7 gold, 1 silver, 2 bronze
Victor Kuzkin – USSR	**9 medals** – 8 gold, 1 silver
Viktor Konovalenko – USSR	**9 medals** – 8 gold, 1 bronze
Sergei Kapustin – USSR	**9 medals** – 7 gold, 1 silver, 1 bronze
Anatoli Firsov – USSR	**8 medals** – 8 gold
Vladimir Vikulov – USSR	**8 medals** – 7 gold, 1 silver

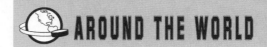
MOST CAREER POINTS AT THE WORLD CHAMPIONSHIP

Boris Mikhailov, USSR	**169**
Valeri Kharlamov, USSR	**159**
Alexander Maltsev, USSR	**156**
Vladimir Petrov, USSR	**154**
Sven Tumba, Sweden	**127**
Sergei Makarov, USSR	**118**
Vladimir Martinec, Czechoslovakia	**110**
Vaniamin Alexandrov, USSR	**104**
Jiri Holik, Czechoslovakia	
Anatoli Firsov, USSR	**101**

GREAT INTERNATIONAL PLAYERS WHO NEVER

Vladislav Tretiak, USSR

Canadian fans first discovered this great goaltender in the 1972 Summit Series between Canada and the Soviet Union. Played in 4 Olympic Games and 13 World Championships. Some would say he was the greatest goalie ever.

Vyacheslav Bykov, USSR / Russia

Bykov had an amazing career in the Soviet Union with the famed Red Army team in Moscow. Won 2 Olympic gold medals and played in 9 World Championships as well as the 1987 Canada Cup.

Ronald Pettersson, Sweden

Pettersson played 252 games for the Swedish national team in every major international tournament between 1955 and 1967.

Valeri Kharlamov, USSR

Was the Soviet offensive star in the 1972 Summit Series. Kharlamov played for the Red Army team in Moscow. He was an Olympic champion twice and world champion 8 times. Died tragically in a car crash when he was only 33 years old.

PLAYED AN NHL GAME

Vladimir Petrov, USSR

Petrov is one of the top scorers in the history of Soviet hockey. He played in the 1972 Summit Series on the Soviets' most dangerous line with Kharlamov and Boris Mikhailov.

Pekka Marjamaki, Finland

Considered one of the top defensemen in the history of Finnish hockey. He played with the national team for 12 years and also won the Finnish League title 5 times.

Leif Holmqvist, Sweden

Was a star in goal with the Swedish National Team from 1962 to 1975. He played 19 games in the World Hockey Association at the end of his career, but never an NHL game.

Jiri Holecek, Czechoslovakia

Long before there was Dominik Hasek, there was Holecek. He was a five-time winner of the Top Goaltender Award at the World Championships.

THE ONLY PLAYERS WHO'VE WON
A WORLD CHAMPIONSHIP, OLYMPIC GOLD AND A STANLEY CUP

Tomas Jonsson	Sweden	**Vladimir Malakhov**	Russia
Hakan Loob	Sweden	**Joe Sakic**	Canada
Mats Naslund	Sweden	**Brendan Shanahan**	Canada
Valeri Kamensky	Russia	**Rob Blake**	Canada
Alexei Gusarov	Russia	**Scott Niedermayer**	Canada
Peter Forsberg	Sweden	**Jaromir Jagr**	Czech Republic
Vyacheslav Fetisov	Russia	**Jiri Slegr**	Czech Republic
Igor Larionov	Russia	**Nicklas Lidstrom**	Sweden
Alexander Mogilny	Russia	**Fredrik Modin**	Sweden

FUN STUFF

Things you will learn on the following pages: scoring on your own team is not a good thing and, no matter what the era, "Old Boot Nose" just doesn't work as a nickname.

SOME OF THE TALLEST PLAYERS

■ Zdeno Chara
2.1 m, 116 kg (6'9", 255 lbs.)
The tallest player in NHL history

■ Hal Gill
2.01 m, 109 kg (6'7", 240 lbs.)
The tallest American-born player
ever to lace 'em up in the NHL

■ Chris McAllister
2.01 m, 107 kg (6'7", 235 lbs.)
Played over 300 games in the
NHL between 1997 and 2004

■ Gilles Lupien
1.98 m, 95 kg (6'6", 210 lbs.)
Known as "The Towering Inferno"

■ Chris Pronger
1.98 m, 100 kg (6'6", 220 lbs.)
Second overall pick in
the 1993 draft

...AND SOME OF THE SHORTEST

■ **Roy "Shrimp" Worters**
1.6 m, 61 kg (5'3", 135 lbs.)
One of the top goalies of his era (1920s–30s)

■ **Bobby Lalonde**
1.65 m, 70 kg (5'5", 155 lbs.)
Played almost 650 games from 1971
to 1982

■ **Darren Pang**
1.65 m, 70 kg (5'5", 155 lbs.)
The second-shortest goalie ever
to play in the NHL

■ **Theoren Fleury**
1.68 m, 82 kg (5'6", 180 lbs.)
Won a Stanley Cup with Calgary
in 1989 and an Olympic gold
medal with Canada in 2002

■ **Henri Richard**
1.7 m, 73 kg (5'7", 160 lbs.)
Hall of Fame centreman won
11 Stanley Cups with
the Montreal Canadiens
between 1955 and 1975

GREAT HOCKEY ARENA SONGS

"Song 2" by Blur

"The Hockey Song" by Stompin' Tom Connors

"We Will Rock You" by Queen

"Celebration" by Kool and the Gang

"Hawaii 5-0" by The Ventures

"50 Mission Cap" by The Tragically Hip

"Try Honesty" by Billy Talent

"Welcome to the Jungle" by Guns 'n' Roses

"Hot In Herre" by Nelly

729 Number of penalty minutes racked up by Dale Hunter during playoff games. Yes, it's a record.

UNUSUAL HOCKEY FASHION STATEMENTS

Sometimes the statement is: "What were they thinking?"

The mullet haircut

Otherwise known as "hockey hair." This is the classic hockey player haircut, feathered on the top, short on the sides and long at the back.

The 1980s Vancouver Canucks sweater

Awful. Black with yellow and orange stripes coming off the shoulder and down to the bottom centre, forming a "V." In the words of their former coach Harry Neale: "We play like clowns some nights, so we may as well dress like them."

The California Seals sweaters and skates

Where do you start? The team was decked out in white skates at one point, gold and green uniforms and, later, teal and gold.

Long hockey pants

In the early 1980s Cooper introduced a hockey pant that came all the way down to the skates (called Cooperalls). They were a little like track pants and they looked ridiculous. The Philadelphia Flyers and the Hartford Whalers both tried the pants out before, mercifully, going back to the traditional look.

Hockey dresses

Back in the mid-1970s many of the New York models who liked to frequent the Rangers' home games at Madison Square Garden would wear an over-sized Rangers sweater as a sort of mini-dress. It may have looked great, but some women complained that "their legs got cold."

GREAT GOALS

These lists are always impossible. You could easily do a list of ten goals each for the game's three greatest players: Bobby Orr, Wayne Gretzky and Mario Lemieux. Which great goals do *you* think have been scored?

Paul Henderson
Canada vs. USSR, September 28, 1972

The eighth, and deciding, game of the Team Canada vs. U.S.S.R. Summit Series. The score was tied 5–5 with less than a minute to play. Phil Esposito dug the puck loose behind the net and passed it out in front to Paul Henderson. Henderson scored with 34 seconds remaining, and Canada won the game 6–5. It is widely regarded as the greatest moment in Canadian sports history.

Bobby Orr
Boston vs. St. Louis, May 10, 1970

The Stanley Cup-winning overtime goal for the Bruins. This famous goal was made even more famous as a result of the photo taken by Ray Lussier that captured Orr in mid-air, arms raised in celebration after he'd fired in the winning goal and been tripped by St. Louis defenseman Noel Picard.

Mike Eruzione
USA vs. USSR, February 22, 1980

It was a semi-final game between the USSR and the USA at the 1980 Winter Olympics in Lake Placid, New York. Nobody gave the group of American college players a chance against the powerhouse Soviets. With the score tied at 3–3 midway through the third period, U.S. captain

Mike Eruzione scored to put the Americans up 4–3. The U.S. held on to eliminate the Soviets, and went on to win the gold medal. It is undoubtedly the greatest moment in U.S. hockey history.

Mario Lemieux
Canada vs. USSR, September 15, 1987

It was the deciding game of the 1987 Canada Cup and, once again, Canada faced the Soviet Union in a classic game. With the score tied 5–5, and under two minutes remaining, the two greatest players of their era combined on this amazing rush which ended with Wayne Gretzky dropping a pass back to Mario Lemieux near the top of the left face-off circle. Lemieux blew a shot past the Soviet netminder with 1:26 remaining to clinch the game, and the tournament, for Canada.

Wayne Gretzky
Edmonton vs. Calgary, April 21, 1988

This is one that doesn't always make lists like this, but will never be forgotten by anyone who witnessed it. It was game two of the Smythe Division championship between bitter rivals Edmonton and Calgary. Edmonton had won the first game of the series and this one went into overtime. At 7:54 of overtime Wayne Gretzky stepped in over the blueline on the left wing and fired a perfect shot past goalie Mike Vernon and into the top corner. Edmonton won the game, the series and, eventually, the Cup. It was the last overtime goal Gretzky would ever score for the Oilers. He was traded to Los Angeles that summer.

BIG HOCKEY BLUNDERS

The 2004–05 Lockout

When players and owners couldn't come to an agreement over a new collective bargaining agreement, owners locked the players out, and an entire season was lost. Has there been a bigger mistake in the history of hockey?

Edmonton defenseman Steve Smith's "own goal"

There was 5:15 to go in the third period of the 7th game of the 1986 Stanley Cup Division Final series between Calgary and Edmonton. The game was tied 2–2 when Oilers' defenseman Steve Smith came out from behind his own net with the puck, and his pass hit the back of goaltender Grant Fuhr's leg and bounced into the Oilers' net. Smith fell to the ice, realizing that he'd just thrown away the game and the series. Calgary won 3–2 and Edmonton was finished.

Tommy Salo Olympian flub

Sweden had what many considered to be the best team at the 2002 Winter Olympics in Salt Lake City, Utah. Sweden, led by Mats Sundin, Daniel Alfredsson, Markus Naslund and Nicklas Lidstrom, were a perfect 3–0–0 after the final round. Then, in their first playoff game against lightly regarded Belarus, disaster struck. A centre-ice flip-in from Vladimir Kopat bounced off the top of Tommy Salo's mask, over his head, down his back and into the net. It was the game winner. Belarus won 4–3 and Sweden was out of the tournament.

Patrick Roy goes Hollywood

Patrick Roy, one of the greatest goalies of all time, certainly had a flair for the dramatic, but this one backfired on him. It was Game 6 of the 2002 Stanley Cup semifinals between Colorado and Detroit. Roy made a nice glove save early in the game on Detroit's Steve Yzerman from point-blank range. Unfortunately, as Roy went to hold his catching glove in the air to add a little flair to the save, the puck flipped out of his glove and into the net. Detroit won the game 2–0.

Missing the empty net

This has happened many times but, thanks to the Internet, Dallas Stars' forward Patrik Stefan has had this embarrassing claim to fame immortalized. Dallas led Edmonton 5–4 late in the third period of a regular season game on January 3, 2007. The Oilers had an empty net, and Stefan had a chance to clinch the victory as he skated with the puck toward the open net. But he missed — from less than a metre away! The Oilers stole the puck and tied the game. Fortunately for Dallas, they ended up winning the game in a shootout.

HOCKEY MOVIES

Some good, some not bad and some just horrible.

Slap Shot, 1977

This classic is considered the best hockey movie ever made. It's about life in the minor leagues and it is very, very funny. Make sure you have your parents' permission before you watch it.

King of Hockey, 1936

The movie was about gamblers who try to get a player to throw a game. It was only 55 minutes long, and they used to show parts of it during *Hockey Night in Canada* intermissions back in the 1970s.

Face-Off, 1971

Its claim to fame was that it featured cameo appearances by several members of the Toronto Maple Leafs and Boston Bruins tough guy Derek Sanderson, among others.

Wayne's World, 1992 and Wayne's World 2, 1993

They're not really hockey movies, but they make the list because of all the hockey references — yelling "Car!" while they're playing street hockey, and then "Game on!" after the car has passed. Also, who could forget Stan Mikita's Donuts?

The Mighty Ducks series (1992, 1994, 1996)

They're all good fun as the "good guys" face-off against the "bad guys." And, yes, it's absolutely true that the team in Anaheim was named after the movie.

Les Boys, 1997 and *Les Boys II,* 1998

Both of these are classics! Some will tell you that, next to *Slap Shot*, these are the two best hockey movies you'll ever see. They've also made III and IV (not as good). All the movies are in French and made in Quebec. They all follow the exploits of a bunch of guys on an amateur hockey team. Good stuff!

Sudden Death, 1995

This big budget Hollywood film stars Jean-Claude Van Damme as the "good guy" trying to rescue the U.S. Vice President from hostage takers at the seventh game of the Stanley Cup Final between the Pittsburgh Penguins and the Chicago Blackhawks. The movie features Van Damme performing martial arts moves in full goalie equipment. Perhaps the worst hockey movie ever made.

Youngblood, 1986

If *Sudden Death* isn't the worst, then *Youngblood* takes the prize. A very young Rob Lowe is a hockey player being pressured to fight to show he can play in the big league. It uses every Canadian hockey cliché in the book, including a love affair between a player and the coach's daughter.

Mystery, Alaska, 1999

Another big budget Hollywood film with a cast that includes Russell Crowe and Burt Reynolds. This film is a little far-fetched — it involves the New York Rangers going to a small town in Alaska to play a challenge match against a local team — but it's heart-warmingly told and quite enjoyable.

MORE GREAT GOALS

Mario Lemieux
New Jersey vs. Pittsburgh, December 31, 1988

It wasn't just one goal, it was five goals scored five different ways. It had never been done before and hasn't been done since. Lemieux scored an even-strength goal, a power-play goal, a shorthanded goal, a goal on a penalty shot and one more, for good measure, into an empty net.

Wayne Gretzky
Philadelphia vs. Edmonton, December 30, 1981

Scoring 50 goals in 50 games is an amazing feat. Maurice "The Rocket" Richard was the first to do it in 1945. Mike Bossy did it 36 years later in 1981. On this night in Edmonton, Gretzky scored five goals and hit the 50 goal mark in an eye-popping 39 games. No player has come close since.

Pete Babando
NY Rangers vs. Detroit, April 23, 1950

Detroit faced the Rangers in game seven of this legendary Stanley Cup Final series, and this was the third game of the series to go into overtime. With the score tied at 3–3, Babando knocked a shot past New York goalie Chuck Rayner at 8:31 of the second overtime period to win the Cup for Detroit.

Guy Lafleur
Boston vs. Montreal, May 10, 1979

It was game seven of the Stanley Cup semi-final series between Montreal and Boston — the two best teams in the league that year. The Bruins led 4–3 with just under two minutes to play when Boston was called for having too many men on the ice. On the resulting powerplay, Guy Lafleur blazed in over the blueline on the right wing and fired an amazing shot that beat Boston goalie Gilles Gilbert on the short side with 1:14 to play. Boston never regained their composure and Montreal won the game and the series in overtime.

Mats Sundin
Sweden vs. USSR, May 4, 1991

The goal by Mats "Sudden" Sundin was scored in the third period of the gold medal game at the 1991 World Hockey Championship to break a 1–1 tie against the Soviets. Sundin skated end to end, coming down the right side of the ice, fighting off a couple of Soviet players before he fired the puck behind the goalie. It was described at the time as one of the greatest goals in Swedish ice hockey.

TEN THINGS YOU'LL FIND IN A TRAINER'S MEDICAL KIT

Found in the kit of Team Canada Spengler Cup trainer Pat Clayton.

✔ Gauze for helping to dress large cuts or scrapes

✔ Tape

✔ Tape cutting scissors

✔ Sterile wound dressing pads

✔ Peroxide wipes (to clean cuts and scrapes)

✔ Topical antibiotic cream

✔ An artificial airway to help someone having difficulty breathing

✔ Liquid bandage

✔ Q-Tips

✔ Alcohol wipes

HOCKEY SONGS

Hockey Night in Canada theme
To Canadians, the most famous hockey tune ever written. The theme to one of the longest running TV sports shows in the world was written in 1968 by a Vancouver-born, classically trained musician named Dolores Claman.

"The Hockey Song"
This little ditty by Canadian folk singer Stompin' Tom Connors was recorded in 1973 and is played at almost every hockey rink in the world. As the song says: "Oh the good ole hockey game is the best game you can name."

"Honky the Christmas Goose"
This classic is sung by former Toronto Maple Leaf and Hall of Fame goalie Johnny Bower. It came out for Christmas 1965 and peaked at number 29 on the hit parade (only 28 spots behind the Beatles' No. 1 "We Can Work it Out").

"Clear the Track, Here Comes Shack"
Recorded by The Secrets in 1966, this rock-and-roll homage to Toronto Maple Leafs' Eddie "The Entertainer" Shack was a No. 1 record.

"Big League"
Canadian rocker Tom Cochrane penned this tune in 1988. It's about a dad who is living his life through his young son who plays hockey.

"Gretzky Rocks"
Of course there has to be a song about the greatest player ever. This one was recorded in 1995 by a band called The Pursuit of Happiness. "Walter Gretzky had a son / He grew up to be the great one." Rock on!

"50 Mission Cap"
This is a great hockey song by a great rock band. This song came out in 1992 and is about Bill Barilko, who scored the Cup-winning goal for the Leafs in 1951. Barilko disappeared that summer in a plane crash. The Leafs didn't win another Cup until 1962, the year Barilko's body was finally discovered.

SOME GREAT HOCKEY NICKNAMES

Maurice **"The Rocket"** Richard

Wayne **"The Great One"** Gretzky

Mario **"The Magnificent"** Lemieux
(also **"Super Mario"** and **"Le Magnifique"**)

Gordie **"Mr. Hockey"** Howe

Patrick **"St. Patrick"** Roy

Bobby **"The Golden Jet"** Hull

Guy **"The Flower"** Lafleur

Howie **"The Stratford Streak"** Morenz

Henri **"The Pocket Rocket"** Richard

Bernie **"Boom Boom"** Geoffrion

Fred **"Cyclone"** Taylor

Dominik **"The Dominator"** Hasek

Curtis **"Cujo"** Joseph

Pavel **"The Russian Rocket"** Bure

Dave **"The Hammer"** Schultz

Yvon **"The Roadrunner"** Cournoyer

Dave **"Tiger"** Williams

Frank **"Mr. Zero"** Brimsek

Stu **"The Grim Reaper"** Grimson

Brett **"The Golden Brett"** Hull

...AND SOME REALLY BAD NICKNAMES

Bert **"Old Pig Iron"** Corbeau

Alf **"The Embalmer"** Pike

Lorne **"Gump"** Worsley

Georges **"The Chicoutimi Cucumber"** Vezina

Jim **"Cement Head"** Hargreaves

Max **"Dipsy-Doodle-Dandy"** Bentley

Rene **"Rainy Drinkwater"** Boileau

Carson **"Shovel Shot"** Cooper

Sid **"Old Boot Nose"** Abel

Eddie **"The Great Gabbo"** Dorohoy

SOME POPULAR NICKNAMES

By far the most popular hockey nicknames are usually made up by either shortening a person's last name (for example "Gretz" or "Espo" for Wayne Gretzky or Phil Esposito), or by adding a letter or two to the last name after you've shortened it (such as "Torts" for John Tortorella) or simply by adding a letter or two to the end of the name (Craig-er, Clarke-y or Cart-s). Go ahead, try it.

"Red"
Used for every guy who's ever played who has red hair ("Red" Storey, "Red" Dutton, "Red" Doran)

"Chief"
Used for years as a nickname for anyone of aboriginal descent (George "Chief" Armstrong, John "Chief" Bucyk)

"Soupy"
Highly imaginative tie-in to the brand of soup for every guy named Campbell

"Moose"
For a big guy ("Moose" Dupont; "Moose" Vasko); variations include Tubby or Porky

"Shrimp"
For a small guy ("Shrimp" Worters); see also: Shorty, Wee or Knobby

MORE BIG BLUNDERS

Pride comes before a fall

It was a classic battle of egos between a new coach and a veteran team leader. Mario Tremblay was the new head coach of the Montreal Canadiens, and Patrick Roy was the veteran team leader. Tremblay's ultimate power-play came on December 2, 1995, when Montreal was hosting Detroit. The Habs were awful, and so was Roy. Halfway through the second period, Roy had let in 9 goals. Finally Roy was pulled from the game. Roy was furious. The Canadiens were forced to trade their star goalie.

The Stamp Goal

It was a sudden-death shootout in the 1994 Olympic gold medal game between Canada and Sweden. Peter Forsberg came in on goal for Sweden, and as he did, he started to drift to his left until his back was completely turned toward the left boards.

Swedish stamp showing Forsberg's goal

Canadian goaltender Corey Hirsch had never seen anything like this. He followed Forsberg across, moving farther away from his goal. But while Forsberg's body was moving toward the side, he trailed his stick, with the puck, behind him and toward the net. As Hirsch slid toward the corner, the puck slid into the empty net. Sweden won the gold and the image was forever preserved one year later on a Swedish postage stamp. Swedes still call it "The Stamp Goal."

FUN STUFF

Kazakhstan defeats Canada

Canada has had some great successes at the World Junior Hockey Championship, but the 1998 tournament wasn't one of them. The Canadians were looking to claim their 6th World Junior Championship in a row. However, things went bad early and finished worse. In their final game against the 1 and 5 Kazakhs, Canada fell behind 4–0 before eventually losing 6–3. It was perhaps Canada's worst-ever effort in the history of the World Juniors.

"Are you sure about that?"

It was a famous case of mistaken identity. Rob Murray was playing his first game for the Winnipeg Jets on November 19, 1992. Murray scored a goal and, as tradition dictates, a teammate, in this case, Teemu Selanne, fished the puck out of the net to give to Murray to commemorate his first NHL goal. The only problem was, Murray had already scored a couple of NHL goals in 58 games with the Washington Capitals. An embarrassed Selanne was heard to remark: "Well, I'm not taking the puck back to the referee."

The 0–0 loss

On December 5, 1925, the Pittsburgh Pirates and the Ottawa Senators were tied 0–0. Ottawa defenseman George Boucher fired the puck toward the Pittsburgh goal when Pirates' player Herb Drury threw his stick to knock the puck away. The rules at the time stated that a penalty was awarded: Ottawa was awarded a goal and won 1–0 with the puck never having entered the net.

Curtis Joseph

NOTABLE GOALIE MASK PAINT JOBS

Gerry Cheevers – Starting in 1968, the Boston Bruins' netminder had stitch marks painted on his mask wherever he was hit by a stick or puck during play. After a few years the mask had a "Frankenstein" quality to it.

Gary Simmons – A colourful goalie from the late '70s who had a giant cobra on his mask in reference to his nickname — "The Cobra."

Ed Belfour – Another nickname reference mask — Eddie "The Eagle" has had variations of an eagle on all of his masks with Chicago, Dallas, Toronto and Florida.

Curtis Joseph – Another great nickname — "Cujo" — and another great mask. This one has the face of a growling, fierce, wild dog (like the one in the Stephen King novel *Cujo*, that Curtis' nickname comes from).

Mike Richter – One of the best designs of the last ten years. Mike had the face of New York's world famous Statue of Liberty on his mask for the 1999–2000 season.

Nikolai Khabibulin – His nickname is "The Bulin Wall," which is a play on "The Berlin Wall" (a huge wall that used to separate East and West Berlin in Germany — look it up). Nikolai's mask has bricks up both sides and his nickname spelled out along the bottom of the mask.

GREAT HOCKEY QUOTES

"Some people skate to the puck. I skate to where the puck is going to be.**"**

— **Wayne Gretzky**

"Hockey belongs on the Cartoon Network, where a person can be pancaked by an ACME anvil, then expanded, accordion-style — back to full stature — without any lasting side effect.**"**

— **American journalist Steve Rushin**

"We get nose jobs all the time in the NHL, and we don't even have to go to the hospital.**"**

— **Brad Park, former NHL defenseman**

"I may be a lot of things, but I'm not dumb enough to be a goalie.**"**

— **former player, and now TV commentator, Brett Hull**

"Last season, we couldn't win at home and we were losing on the road. My failure as a coach was that I couldn't think of any place else to play.**"**

— **former Vancouver Canucks' coach Harry Neale on his failings as a bench boss**

"Only in America."

— Miroslav Satan, on getting asked
whether or not that is his real name
every time he tries to use his credit card

"Part of the learning curve in Edmonton is learning to hate Calgary."

— former Oilers defenseman Steve Smith
on the great Flames-Oilers rivalry

"You're playing worse every day and right now you're playing like the middle of next week."

— the late, great coach Herb Brooks speaking
to the team that eventually won the 1980
Olympic ice hockey gold medal

"How would you like a job where, every time you make a mistake, a big red light goes on and 18,000 people boo?"

— Hall of Fame goaltender Jacques Plante,
speaking to a reporter about the tough
part of being an NHL goalie

HOCKEY QUOTES FROM TV AND MOVIES

❝ Okay, Marge, it's your child against my child. The winner will be showered with praise. The loser will be taunted and booed until my throat is sore. ❞

— **Homer Simpson,** *The Simpsons*

❝ Now here's the long and short of it: I hate hockey and I don't like kids. ❞

— **coach Gordon Bombay,** *The Mighty Ducks*

❝ This is hockey, okay? It's not rocket surgery. ❞

— **Donnie Shulzhoffer,** *Mystery, Alaska*

57,167 Number of people who made up the record NHL crowd on November 22, 2003, at Edmonton's Commonwealth Stadium for the outdoor game between the Edmonton Oilers and the Montreal Canadiens

" Hey, Goldberg! I'll bet if that puck were a cheeseburger you'd stop it. **"**

— opposing player to Mighty Ducks goalie, *Mighty Ducks 2*

" He's hit his head on the ice. He hit it so hard his kids will be born dizzy. **"**

— play-by-play announcer, *Sudden Death*

" Would you rather spread manure, or play hockey in Madison Square Garden in front of 18,000 people? **"**

— farmer father Kelly Youngblood to his son, *Youngblood*

" You're crazy. Me? Ha! I'm not the one paying some Neanderthal 40 million dollars a year to skate up and down the ice. **"**

— a Secret Service agent to a team owner, *Sudden Death*

" If it's a boy, I want to call him Saku. **"**

— Mario proclaims his loyalty to Canadiens captain Saku Koivu in the movie *Les Boys*

143

HOCKEY NAMES THAT DON'T QUITE CUT IT

Calgary Flames — The franchise inherited the name from the Atlanta Flames — which made sense (the Great Atlanta Fire of 1917). There has been no Great Fire in Calgary.

Montreal Maroons — A team named after a colour. What can you say?

Mighty Ducks of Anaheim — A professional hockey team named after a kids' movie?

Kokudo Bunnies — A Japanese team where Canadian Olympian and Edmonton Oilers great Randy Gregg played for a season. In his words: "It was a challenge to look intimidating in a jersey with a big picture of a bunny rabbit on the front."

Lewiston MAINEiacs — Get it? The Quebec Major Junior Hockey League team is located in Lewiston, Maine. Funny and clever, isn't it? Well, maybe not . . .

Oakland Seals — Later to become the California Golden Seals before finally bidding *adieu* to the name when the franchise moved to Cleveland. There are indeed seals off the coast of California, but they have nothing to do with hockey.

Amarillo Gorillas — Played in the Central Hockey League for one season. Amarillo is a city in the fine state of Texas where the only gorillas to be found are in a zoo.

TOUGHEST PLAYERS IN THE NHL *

Georges Laraque

Derek Boogaard

Donald Brashear

Zdeno Chara

Scott Parker

Chris Chelios

Colton Orr

Jarome Iginla

Chris Neil

Tomas Holmstrom

* source: ESPN Player Survey

SLANG TERMS EVERY HOCKEY FAN

Dump and chase
"They're playing dump and chase hockey."

When a team fires the puck into the corners in the offensive zone and then goes after it; the opposite of carrying the puck into the zone.

Goon
"That guy's a goon!"

A player whose main "skill" is fighting.

Lit up
"We really lit him up."

When a team scores a lot of goals against a goalie; refers to the red goal-light going on.

Lumber or twig
"Hey, pass me a new twig, will ya."

Slang terms for a hockey stick.

Saucer pass
"He saucers that puck across to Jones."

A pass that goes in the air, over sticks, legs etc., and lands flat on the ice.

SHOULD KNOW

Filled in
"He's been filled in."

When a player is on the bad end of a big hit.

Fed
**"He fed him a nice pass" or
"He fed him about five punches."**

Passing the puck or getting badly beaten in a fight.

Barn
"We beat them in their own barn."

Rink or arena.

Lord Stanley's Mug or Stanley
"Is Stanley in the building right now?"

Slang terms for the Stanley Cup.

Suicide pass
"He fed him a suicide pass."

A pass requiring the receiver to gain control of the puck while skating toward an oncoming forward or defenseman from the other team; quite often ends up with the receiver getting filled in (see above).

INDEX